Clarity Competes

"Why the Future Belongs to Leaders Who Align Cost, Culture, and Innovation"

Asim Kumar Mukhopadhyay

STARDOM BOOKS

www.StardomBooks.com

STARDOM BOOKS
112 Bordeaux Ct.
Coppell, TX 75019, USA

FIRST EDITION MARCH 2026

STARDOM BOOKS, LLC.
112 Bordeaux Ct. Coppell, TX 75019, USA

www.stardombooks.com

Stardom Books
United States and India

Clarity Competes
*"Why the Future Belongs to Leaders Who
Align Cost, Culture, and Innovation"*

Asim Kumar Mukhopadhyay

p. 176
cm. 13.97 X 21.59

Category: BUS025000 Business & Economics : Entrepreneurship
BUS071000 Business & Economics : Leadership

ISBN : 978-1-957456-89-8

Dedication

This book is for leaders who choose discipline over noise,
And long-term value over short-term applause.
And to the teams who make leadership real, not through titles,
But through everyday decisions that quietly shape the future.

Acknowledgments

This book is the outcome of years spent working alongside leaders, teams, and organizations navigating complexity, constraint, and change. I am deeply grateful to the many colleagues, mentors, and partners who shaped my thinking not through theory, but through real decisions made under real pressure.

I owe particular thanks to the leadership teams and frontline professionals across industries who allowed me to learn from their challenges, experiments, and successes. Their openness and discipline form the backbone of this work.

I am grateful to my peers and advisors who challenged my assumptions, sharpened my arguments, and pushed me toward greater coherence in thought and execution.

This book would be incomplete without Stardom's team.

Finally, I thank my family, my wife, Indrani, and my daughter, Trinanjana, for their patience, support, and quiet encouragement throughout this journey. Their steadiness made this work possible.

Contents

Foreword — *i*

Endorsements — *iii*

Introduction — *ix*

1. The Cost–Value Paradox — *1*

2. Building a Precision Mindset — *25*

3. Frameworks for Strategic Cost Competitiveness — *47*

4. The Innovation Multiplier — *71*

5. Competing in The Indian Context — *91*

6. Technology as a Force Multiplier — *109*

7. People, Culture, and Competitive Edge — *127*

8. The Future-Ready Enterprise — *141*

Conclusion — *151*

About the author — *153*

Foreword

Leaders have learned an important lesson over the last decade: complexity is growing faster than capability. Markets are more irrational than we remain solvent, technology evolves faster than planning cycles, and organisations juggle more priorities than they can manage. In such an environment, clarity becomes essential for survival.

This is why Clarity Competes resonated with me from the start. What Asim has crafted is not another book on operational excellence or innovation theory—it is a grounded, experience-rich articulation of a challenge leaders confront daily: ensuring that the many moving parts of an enterprise do not drift in different directions.

Having worked across technology, finance, and manufacturing, I have seen firsthand how misalignment stems not from a lack of intelligence but from a disconnect between organisations and the environments they operate in. I've witnessed a highly successful cost intervention that unintentionally killed future product pipelines; a promising technology initiative stalled because organisational culture was unprepared for it; and numerous quality outputs from capable teams that ultimately produced little impact.

Asim brings together cost, culture, technology, and innovation with clarity. His reframing of cost analysis is particularly powerful. While many treat cost as a constraint, Asim positions it as a deliberate design parameter—enabling organisations to build agility rather than defaulting to austerity.

Technology deployment suffers from similar misconceptions. I have long believed in the potential of digital ecosystems, yet I see how often technology is deployed broadly without purpose.

Asim's principles—Precision before Platforms and Value before Volume—are among the sharpest arguments I've encountered, reminding us that tools must elevate judgement, not replace it.

His pragmatism stands out: real examples, applicable frameworks, and a contextual understanding of how digital leadership intersects with manufacturing from an Indian perspective. His discussion of coherence—a gap many leaders feel but seldom articulate—captures how functional disconnects and execution gaps often erode the brilliance of individual contributors.

By giving this challenge language and structure, Asim provides leaders with a practical pathway toward what I see as the biggest differentiator in modern enterprises: the ability to think and act as one system.

For leaders driving transformation, Clarity Competes offers what I value most in leadership writing: perspective, practicality, and a mindset shift that endures. It reminds us that clarity is not about simplifying the world, but strengthening organisations to thrive in one that is only growing more complex.

- P.B. Balaji
CEO, Jaguar Land Rover (JLR)

Endorsements

Many a times in industries such as energy. utilities, and infrastructure. Successful outcomes are very tangible- pipelines, networks, and project completion. However, this view offers no insight into the complexity of decision-making in a rapidly changing environment, including making uncertain decisions and fluctuating costs. disruptive technologies, and the difficulty of bringing teams from across multiple disciplines, geographies, and time zones together.

Clarity, therefore, is a requirement rather than just a virtue of good leadership in this environment. ***Clarity Competes*** impressed me with how deftly Asim Kumar Mukhopadhyay defines the unseen aspect of leadership. This unseen aspect is one of alignment rather than ambition; it is what determines the ultimate success or failure of any organization over time.

In my experience across industry, I have seen several companies fail, not necessarily because they lacked talented or dedicated employees. Every employee uses their own definition of the company's objectives to inform their decisions, which creates distinct variations in team decision-making.

Asim's book addresses this gap with clarity and practicality. His ability to integrate cost, culture, technology, and innovation into a single system is one of the things I admire most about him. His view of these elements as part of a living system supports the idea that success in a complex, large-scale organization depends on how individuals' capabilities interact, rather than on their capabilities alone.

Asim has argued that Cost is Capability: Precision is Culture; Technology is Purpose: and Coherence is Competitive Advantage.

These are consistent with the experiences of executives running large-scale businesses. In addition to these insights, Asim's work provides a valuable resource from an Indian perspective. The challenges faced by leaders in India are distinct, given the country's multifaceted diversity, aspirations, resource constraints, and policy transformation. and enormous opportunities. Western structures do not apply to the Indian market, and leaders must understand their context more precisely: respect their operational realities; and strike a balance between frugality and ambition. Asim's work demonstrates this balance through his understanding of the subjects and through his compassion for others.

Clarity Competes does not prescribe or dictate; it does not offer simple approaches or "one-size-fits-all" lists of things to accomplish, but instead provides several broad-based mental constructs (or mental models) to assist in creating thoughtful, mission-aligned decisions. These mental models allow leaders to identify and address misinterpretations and/or mistakes they may have encountered but cannot articulate. In this age of accelerated change and greater sophistication, Clarity Competes will serve as an informed point of reference for business leaders across all sectors. To be clear, Clarity Competes does not simply guide leaders to respond to disruption with intelligence; it helps them create companies that continuously generate value, even in an uncertain environment.

For policymakers, industry leaders, young professionals, and anyone else responsible for shaping the future of enterprise in India. Clarity Competes will offer a perspective that is both highly relevant and necessary.

- S.K. Gupta
Ex-Chairman & Managing Director, GAIL

In ***Clarity Competes***, Asim Kumar Mukhopadhyay presents an integrated perspective on modern competitiveness, showing why cost, value, innovation, technology, culture, and adaptability cannot be managed in isolation. The book's strength lies in its systems-oriented approach, guiding leaders to move beyond fragmented initiatives and build coherence across decisions, behaviours, and organisational priorities.

Rooted in practical experience and closely attuned to the Indian business context, it provides leaders with a system-level framework to align resources, processes, and people effectively. For those seeking discipline, clarity, and sustainable competitive advantage, 'Clarity Competes' offers a structured and insightful guide for leading complex organisations with purpose and confidence. It equips leaders to translate strategy into consistent results, foster innovation without losing operational discipline, and build organisations that are resilient, adaptable, and future-ready.

- B Thiagarajan
Managing Director, Blue Star Limited

From the several transformation projects I have witnessed, ranging from the restructuring of traditional industrial companies to the rapid expansion of digital native firms, one common factor has emerged: Companies do not typically fail due to a lack of intelligence or motivation; they typically struggle because the different parts of the organization do not work together. The organization's Strategy may say one thing, its Processes reward something else, its Culture acts thirdly, and Technology attempts to connect the often unconnectable dots.

This is why **Clarity Competes** by Asim Mukhopadhyay feels so timely and essential. The book goes beyond frameworks and buzzwords to address the fundamental constraint in modern leadership: the ability to create coherence in an increasingly fragmented world. Leaders who will succeed in the next decade are not those who simply react to change, but those who build organizations where cost, culture, technology, and innovation reinforce one another by choice and by design.

- *Rajat Dhawan*
Senior Managing Partner, India
McKinsey & Company

Clarity Competes is a unique management book that provides an integrated, system-level view of the sustained advantage that companies build instead of fragmented advice. Asim Kumar Mukhopadhyay, who brings us to the frontline realities of the business world instead of abstract theory, convinces us that cost, culture, innovation, technology, and strategy must all be designed as one single operating philosophy. The main insight of the book is both simple and powerful: competitive advantage today is less about isolated excellence and more about coherence in decisions and execution. I especially appreciate how it reinterprets cost as a strategic capability, technology as a deliberate advantage, and culture as the fuel of execution which are ideas that strongly resonate with India's resource-poor, fast-paced context. The frameworks and mental models introduced here will be instantly helpful to CXOs, entrepreneurs, and educators. This is a practical, thoughtful, and well-timed contribution that will assist leaders in transitioning from activity to alignment and from complexity to clarity.

- Dr. Amit Karna

Professor Strategy IIM Ahmedabad

Few books capture India's complexity with such grounded realism—where constraints, scale, speed, and aspiration collide daily. The author presents a disciplined, leadership-led framework that integrates cost, innovation, technology, and culture into a coherent operating system. Essential for Indian leaders, valuable across global markets.

- Ajay S Patil

CFO and Independent Director

Introduction

If there is one pattern I have seen across industries, geographies, and company sizes, it is this: most organizations don't struggle because they lack resources. They struggle because they lack clarity.

I have walked through spotless factories where every machine hummed in perfect rhythm, yet teams worked in silent confusion because priorities were unclear. I have been in boardrooms where capable leaders passionately agreed on a decision, only to execute five different interpretations of it. I have seen start-ups with bold vision collapse because they couldn't translate ambition into daily discipline, and legacy companies lose competitiveness through a series of small, unresolved misalignments.

Eventually, the real issue becomes obvious: misalignment.

- Teams move in different directions.
- Functions pursue different goals.
- Leaders speak different languages.

The result is not only financial loss; it is wasted energy, delayed decisions, inconsistent experiences, and eroded trust. Yet these costs rarely show up in a spreadsheet:

- Approvals stall because no one knows who the decision-maker is
- Rework rises because the first version wasn't aligned
- Innovation slows because people fear ambiguity
- Customers leave not due to product failure but due to inconsistent experiences

The costs of confusion compound quietly... until they threaten competitiveness.

This book is rooted in one fundamental premise: confusion, not cost, is the real enemy of business performance.

When organizations cannot see where value is created or lost, they default to cutting expenses. But without clarity, cost-cutting often:

- Weakens capability rather than sharpening focus
- Damages culture rather than building ownership
- Slows innovation rather than improving discipline

They trim muscle instead of fat. Clarity, in contrast, strengthens the three levers that shape every organization's future:

Clarity aligns:

- **Cost discipline:** spend where value is created and stop where it isn't
- **Culture of trust:** people know what matters and are empowered to act
- **Innovation momentum:** constraints drive creativity instead of fear

This alignment is why the future belongs to clarity-driven leaders.

Innovation is often treated as glamorous, reserved for labs and big budgets. But every breakthrough I've seen was born from:

- **Constraints**
- **Focus**
- **Cross-functional clarity**

When teams know what problem they are solving and what value they are creating, innovation becomes pragmatic rather than performative. Technology follows the same rule: Technology doesn't create clarity. Clarity makes technology valuable. Digital transformation without clarity is just expensive confusion.

We are entering a decade defined by disruption, economic volatility, climate pressures, demographic shifts, and accelerating technologies. The winners will not be the fastest or the biggest, but the best aligned.

They will:

- Anticipate instead of react
- Redesign instead of a patch
- Simplify instead of complicating

Adaptability, powered by clarity, will define competitive advantage.

Why I Wrote This Book

Across decades of working with organizations, I realized a universal truth:

- Cost competitiveness is not a financial problem
- Innovation is not an R&D problem
- Culture is not an HR problem
- Technology is not an IT problem
- Future readiness is not a strategy problem

Every business problem eventually becomes a leadership problem. And every leadership problem eventually becomes a clarity problem.

This book provides leaders with a cohesive lens to connect cost, value, precision, culture, technology, and innovation into a single integrated operating model.

Because when organizations operate without integration, they drift. When they operate with clarity, they transform.

What You Will Gain

Rather than formulas or theories, this book offers something more powerful:

- A way of thinking
- A way of seeing misalignment early
- A way of questioning assumptions
- A way of aligning priorities and actions
- A way of designing for resilience and growth

It will help you:

- Reduce waste without reducing value
- Strengthen culture while improving performance
- Innovate with discipline and direction
- Use technology properly
- Build adaptability into your operating model

There are no silver bullets, hacks, or shortcuts promised in this book. Instead, it offers a type of lucidity that develops gradually. Over time, it improves choices, systems, culture, and strategy. Organizations flourish when leaders genuinely and consistently embrace these values. The future belongs to leaders who align their spending, how their people work, and where innovation truly matters. And clarity is how we get there.

Thank you for choosing to begin this journey.

Chapter 1
The Cost–Value Paradox

It's easy to be excited when you're a company that has cut its operating costs by 30% in just one year. Employees should feel proud of this accomplishment, and investors are likely to appreciate the increased profits. This excitement is often reflected in the number of press announcements the company makes during this period. This initial excitement can quickly evaporate, however, as customers begin to leave and employees become increasingly disengaged from the company's vision. By the end of the company's next fiscal year, analysts expect its market share to be down 40% from its pre-cost-cutting level.

What went wrong? On paper, the company looked more efficient than ever. But behind the numbers, the real story was unfolding; value to the customer had quietly evaporated.

Across industries, there is a paradox. Jet Airways was an example of this paradox: the airline took shortcuts to save costs, lost customers, and went out of business. Kingfisher Airlines impressed the market for a time before losing out due to its inability to sustain its cost structure. In 2009, GM was bailed out after many decades of dominance in the industry due to its inability to compete globally in the long term. In addition, British Airways, a luxury airline with a reputation for quality, lost its customer base after it began to prioritize cost over service. In India, BSNL and MTNL, previously government-run monopolies, were unable to keep pace with the private sector and lost customers because they could not be both efficient and innovative.

While cutting expenses is essential, it is not the end in itself. Reducing costs can be dangerous, as many companies today claim they are "leaner" or have "improved their margins." However, the accurate measure of success is whether customers, employees, and the marketplace see and feel value from your business. A company that reduces costs but loses credibility is no different from a marathon runner who gets out of the blocks well but never finishes the race.

The more interesting and vital point this book explores is the relationship between cost and value. Cost and value are not adversaries; they complement each other. Leaders must learn to master both cost and value simultaneously. Waste is something to eliminate; Whereas earning worth is absolutely imperative to business success.

As severe as the warning may be, there's a greater opportunity for growth and success if you avoid shortcuts; instead, you will endure sustainable growth. Companies that thrive through disruption build strong customer loyalty; they do not merely cut costs. Innovative companies consider cost discipline as their foundation for innovation, trust, and value creation.

Balancing Cost Reduction and Value Creation

Every business feels the pressure to reduce costs. Margins are thin, competition is fierce, and the temptation to cut costs quickly is always present. Yet, as experience shows, the way an organization pursues cost reduction makes all the difference between incremental survival and exponential growth. The correct pressure comes when the value of cost reductions (which can be a legitimate approach to creating value) is assessed as an end in itself.

We've all observed in organizations the short-term cost reductions achieved by acting opportunistically, reducing employee benefits, or otherwise seeking to extract "value" from their products without considering the powerful implications of mutual cost-reducing behaviors. More often than not, these things are downward spirals: a decline in quality, a decline in trust, and ultimately a decline in competitiveness.

The alternative is strategic cost management, a life-cycle perspective that goes beyond quick wins to create sustained advantage. Every rupee saved should be redirected toward innovation, capability building, and market advantage. In this model, cost discipline fuels growth rather than undermines it.

The way two methods that are viewed as similar are different in implementation. Jugaad, or democratic innovation, has created short-term success and immediate benefits by solving problems and creating opportunities; however, it tends to foster a false perception of competitive advantage. The precision-based leadership approach removes waste from an industry's value stream, recycling it into the stream for value and creating opportunities to develop quality and differentiation within it. The definition of precision is optimizing investments to achieve an organization's aspirational, longer-term goals rather than making investments based on over- or under-investment at that time.

To succeed, the challenge is not just to beat the competition with lower prices, as in Make in India and Make for India, but also to produce at global levels of quality. By working to maximize our price-quality gaps, companies can create a positive feedback loop on their operating costs (the price of creating products) through continuous improvement of customer-driven innovations associated with waste removal and through sustainable expansion of competitiveness in the marketplace.

Cost savings without Value Generation cannot last, but together they create greater benefit than the two separately.

Strategic leaders do not only ask "Where can we save on costs?" but also "Where can we build up our value?" The true power of costs isn't reducing them; it's investing the savings from reduced costs in developing new competencies that customers value and reward.

Cost or Value

In many companies, cost and value are represented on opposite sides of a scale. As cost decreases, so does value. Therefore, when faced with margin pressures, leaders often think they must choose between cost efficiency and value excellence. This thinking may explain why many companies view cost reductions as quick fixes (100m sprints) rather than long-term (marathon).

This kind of reasoning is also dangerous because it doesn't take into account that acting foolishly can have both negative long-term consequences and immediate fringe benefits, but only at the expense of future costs. There will likely be times when short-term gains result from cost eliminations; however, these gains will always come at the cost of long-term damage to a company's brand and reputation, employee morale and engagement, and employee trust in management.

The problem is not cost reduction itself but the approach: "Some organizations that don't believe in a balanced perspective, a life-cycle perspective, go for cost-cutting without a value proposition. That creates the problem."

There are three types of cost-reduction strategies: quick wins, tactical, and strategic. Quick wins can work in certain urgent situations, but they cannot be used as a sustainable solution for long-term competitive advantage.

Tactical cuts, if done correctly, can help increase company efficiency. While strategic cuts go deeper, eliminating waste and capturing value, they also create a new advantage.

While working at the steel plant, I noticed large stacks of limestone being accumulated in a designated disposal area. These piles were growing steadily, occupying space and being treated as unavoidable waste. Curious, I enquired into the reason and was told that this limestone had a very high silica content, which made it unsuitable for its intended application and therefore unusable under existing operating assumptions.

Instead of accepting this classification at face value, I decided to make a deep dive, examine its chemical composition, and review how silica interacts with the blast furnace process. What emerged was a counterintuitive insight: although the high-silica limestone could not be used conventionally, it could be charged into the blast furnace in controlled proportions by partially replacing quartzite, as it can contribute to the slag in place of quartzite. While this resulted in a lower yield, it did not impair metallurgical quality or downstream performance.

The trade-off was clear and acceptable. By rethinking the application rather than rejecting the material outright, we could convert what was considered waste into a usable input, reduce disposal volumes, and improve overall material efficiency. This experience stayed with me because it reinforced an early lesson I have carried throughout my career: waste often exists not because materials lack value, but because thinking lacks precision. When leaders question assumptions and examine constraints closely, they often uncover value hidden in plain sight.

While this was not a quick fix, it was the process of moving from tactical to strategic and turning surplus into opportunity. The experience demonstrated that, ultimately, being competitive is not just about elimination but about having a strategy to rethink processes and uncover hidden value.

There is a longstanding belief that cost and value must always pull in opposite directions. This belief is false. Effective leaders reject false dichotomies and design strategies that use cost discipline to create value. The concept of cost and value being held against each other applies across industries; it is clearly visible in steel and in the automobile industry. Organizations that incorporate this lesson into their own business designs move from fragile to durable competitiveness.

The Dangers of Single-Dimensional Cost Cutting

One-dimensional cost-cutting may seem quick, easy, and appealing in today's economic environment, as many leaders experience rising sales volume, lower operating costs, and higher profit margins through cost reduction.

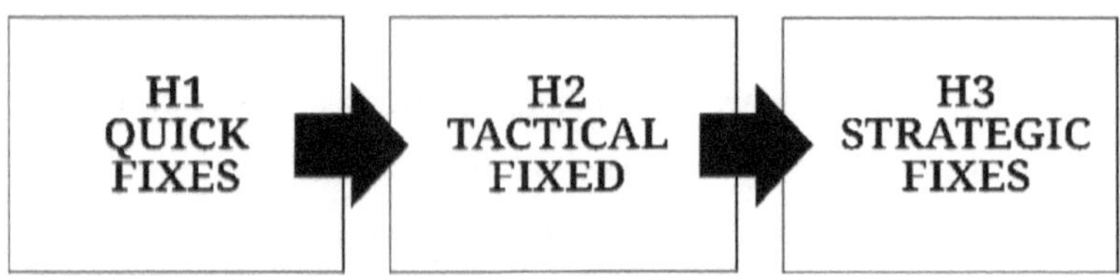

While these leaders are enjoying the monetary rewards from shareholders, the relief from budgetary stress is likely premature; cutting costs alone does not improve profits; cutting costs without also focusing on value can erode a company's competitive advantage.

A common misperception among many executives is that businesses operate similarly to 100-meter sprints. This notion of fast hits leads people to abandon long-term strategies for short-term gains. Quick wins ultimately lead to extinction because they lack long-term sustainability. The only way to create long-term sustainability is through constant improvement.

Business failure stories show how organizations that only see costs are missing out on the value-balancing lever they could use to enhance their value proposition. Jet Airways was one of India's top carriers but began cutting services to save costs. The cost savings were apparent on paper but caused irreparable, long-term damage. Trust was lost as the customer experience declined and loyalty weakened, leading to a collapse in their competitive position before their financials reflected it.

Kingfisher Airlines demonstrated how glamour, aggressive pricing, and bold marketing can create excitement, but its business model lacked sustainable cost controls and failed to deliver value. Its risks did not prevent the accumulation of debt, operational problems, or the loss of customer trust. What initially appeared to be a daring strategy ultimately proved harmful. Likewise, General Motors faced issues in its international markets, reflecting broader problems within the U.S. auto industry. While Toyota and Honda introduced innovative, evolving vehicle lines in the 1990s and 2000s, GM's products remained outdated, leading to a shrinking market share and a bailout in 2009. Merely improving efficiency is insufficient; without innovation, prospects remain limited. British Airways' decline from the late 1990s to early 2000s illustrates a different pattern. Pursuing profits, it compromised its reputation as a top-tier global airline, while rising competition from airlines like Emirates and Singapore Airlines accelerated its decline. Cost-cutting measures reduced customer value.

Meanwhile, India's BSNL and MTNL serve as cautionary tales. Once dominant with near-monopoly status, they failed to keep pace with changing customer expectations and innovative private competitors such as Jio and Airtel, whose strategies prioritized technological advancement and added value. Their focus on cost reduction over innovation and customer needs led to rapid obsolescence in a competitive environment.

When looking at each of these instances, the general trend is that cost reduction alone does not provide an organization with sustained competitiveness; rather, it contributes to a decline in competitiveness. When companies use cost as a constraint rather than a strategic advantage, they risk losing the value their customers, employees, and the marketplace expect them to create. It takes much more than just a focus on reducing costs to secure a sustainable competitive advantage; organizations must successfully tie their costs to innovation, customer experience, and the long-term strategic direction of their business.

The Ripple Effects of Blind Cost Cutting

The far-reaching implications of "cutting costs without proper evaluation" can severely impact an organization beyond the balance sheet.

Cost reduction has the most immediate impact on product and service quality. As companies replace reliable components with lower-quality alternatives and refine or eliminate systems that ensure consistency, Customers will not see these declines from day one. Nevertheless, customers always see the outcome here. As few compromises are made, and reliability declines, the brand's reputation/crisis potential will erode.

The same potential impact that "cutting costs without logical reasoning" has on product/service quality is felt by employees within the organization.

Employee pride comes when they build, sell, or service a quality product/service. However, employees see the organization eliminate key elements that build its reputation or sacrifice product/service quality to reduce profits, which ultimately leads to reduced employee morale. When employee morale is diminished, productivity and accountability also decrease. While businesses can eventually regain their profits, restoring employee confidence is far more difficult. For instance, when an organization loses a significant amount of market share, this loss creates a mental perception (mental scar) for employees, making it difficult to repair, especially since, as consumers, they were also affected by that loss of reputation.

The next victim of the above factors will be the brand itself. Strong Brands are built over time through a painstaking process, and once established, a strong Brand reputation can quickly erode when cost-cutting affects the Customer's experience. Brands may quickly gain or lose their premium status based on how they are built and marketed. British Airways has lost its status as a premier airline worldwide. They are a classic case of how a Carrier can lose its identity by losing touch with its customers and failing to differentiate itself from other Carriers.

The ultimate consequence of all these factors will be Customer attrition. With so many options available to Consumers today and Consumer lethargy at an all-time high, if a brand provides a poor experience, the Consumer will leave quickly. A minimal decrease in the consistency of Service or Quality Products will immediately create a very adverse Customer reaction. This adverse reaction creates a domino effect, starting with Customer dissatisfaction, followed by

Customer switching, and, lastly, Customer advocacy against the Brand. A minor erosion of a Customer's Loyalty can turn into a downward spiral for a company's revenues and significantly weaken its competitive position.

The ramifications of poor Service are not abstract. This means the ramifications are immediate, measurable, and, in many cases, irreversible. Cost reductions that occur during this Cost-Reduction Race result in burning out a company's competitiveness before it gets to the finish line. The only way for companies to demonstrate their competitiveness is not by sprinting to create the lowest cost. It is by pacing all related costs toward the ultimate goal of Value Creation.

Just as a marathon requires endurance, discipline, and foresight to be successful, so too do sustainable businesses take a long view of their business models and consider all that goes into producing a product over its life cycle (rather than just the current quarter). Sustainable companies typically make investments that ultimately pay off in dividends, sometimes after years of hard work, creating a reputation and resilience along the way.

By refocusing their business operations on the "marathon" concept rather than a single-minded focus on cost-cutting, leaders gain a better understanding of what makes their business successful. Businesses will now look beyond immediate cost savings and consider the long-term vitality of their brand, employees, and customers.

Many companies have fallen victim to the exact root cause: they take cost-cutting measures without considering how those cost-cutting measures will affect customer value, operational strength, or future capabilities. Jet Airways and BSNL did not fail due to poor motives; rather, their failures stemmed from cost-cutting measures implemented independently and not as part of an integrated approach.

The reason these companies failed is that they used cost-cutting as an emergency measure rather than a planned, well-thought-out strategy; therefore, they lost competitiveness in the future to gain temporary relief. In the short run, a budget may appear to be in good shape (for a few quarters), but as the organization continues to cut costs, it loses capabilities; service levels deteriorate, trust erodes, and it becomes more difficult to recover from each subsequent cycle of cost-cutting. The failure is not in implementing cost-cutting measures; it is in failing to define what creates future competitiveness. Future sustainable competitiveness cannot be achieved through shortcuts; it is built over time through sound and rational business decisions.

The Importance of Strategically Leveraging Cost

Throughout my career, I have viewed costs as a catalyst for growth rather than an expense. Cost should serve purpose. It should be saved and reinvested into R&D, building capabilities, improving customer focus, etc. Another question is how to redirect those resources to build resilience and strengthen the Company's competitive position. The focus of cost management is not simply to reduce costs; rather, it is to maximize the Company's ability to utilize its resources and generate additional value that will fuel increases in sales and profit.

It has been my long-standing belief that any cost is valuable only if it enables reinvestment in growth. Every time I have been involved with a cost program, I have asked myself a basic set of questions: Will it enable us to innovate? Will it enable us to develop our capabilities? Will it enable us to be closer to our customers? If the answer to any of these questions is no, the savings resulting from the cost program will not be worth pursuing.

Cost should never be a blunt instrument; instead, it should be used like a scalpel. When used properly, a scalpel will remove the unnecessary whilst leaving the strong intact and oftentimes enhanced.

One significant difference between wasteful cutting and careful reduction is precision. Early in my career, I was struck by how easily organizations could mislead themselves through approximate costing systems. Traditional absorption costing, while convenient, often spreads overheads using broad averages such as machine hours or labor hours. On paper, this looks rigorous. In reality, it masks actual cost behavior and distorts pricing decisions.

The consequence is subtle but dangerous. Products that should be competitive are priced out of the market, while others quietly destroy margins. Over time, market share erodes not because of poor products, but because leaders are making decisions based on blurred cost signals.

This realization fundamentally changed how I viewed cost. Precision in costing is not an accounting exercise; it is a strategic necessity. Without understanding what truly drives cost at the activity level, organizations are left estimating rather than knowing—and estimates have a habit of failing under competitive pressure.

To accurately estimate an item's total cost, it is essential to understand its total life-cycle cost and to convince the customer of the concept of Total Cost of Ownership (TCO). Whenever I've told my colleagues to pay a higher price at the beginning so they would have better value later, I have always used an Air Conditioning System as an example. On day one, a unit with a more energy-efficient compressor will cost more than a unit with a conventional compressor. Still, by the end of its life, you will have saved way more than you would have if you had purchased the unit with the conventional compressor.

As we move forward, adopting a subscription-based model for the majority of our services and goods, the idea of considering cost from a 'Total Life Value Perspective' will become increasingly important, rather than simply focusing on the upfront cost.

The fundamental question I ask when evaluating a financial option based on cost is: Will lowering this cost increase or enhance the value for my customer? **If the answer is "no,"** then I have not made the right decision. While it is easy to cut costs, that is not the right way to respect the customer's trust, safety, and consistent service reliability. A perfect example of this would be changing an all-metal part for a low-cost plastic substitute. While this is a wise decision on paper, the long-term impacts far exceed any immediate savings.

Genuine cost leadership does not mean cutting back on quality; instead, it means eliminating unnecessary costs while providing as much, or more, value to the customer. Genuine cost leadership is an ongoing process - a discipline - that builds both the organization and its customers.

When organizations view cost as a means of strategic advantage, everything changes. Instead of limiting organizations, cost becomes the source of their advantage. The right tools provide transparent visibility into actual costs within an organization, reinvestment channels convert costs into profit, and the value retained test ensures that customers are at the center of what an organization does. Cost becomes more than a line item on an expense report; it becomes an organization's competitive advantage.

Competitive Cost-plus Differentiated Value

Over the years, I have learned that cost by itself is never enough. You may manage costs brilliantly, but if you fail to create differentiated value for your customers, your competitiveness will not last.

On the other hand, value alone without cost discipline cannot be sustained; the business will eventually collapse under pressure.

When these two forces come together, however, the impact is transformational. Efficient cost structures protect margins and make the company resilient in downturns. Differentiated value gives customers a reason to stay loyal and to pay attention even in crowded markets. Together, they create a sustainable competitive advantage.

Why the Combination Creates Sustainable Advantage

The test of leadership is whether an organization can deliver more value per unit of cost. A competitive cost structure enables a company to remain efficient, disciplined, and future-ready. Differentiated value ensures that what we deliver is not a commodity but something unique and rewarding for the customer.

When businesses focus solely on reducing costs, they become inflexible. If businesses operate only for value while ignoring how costs affect them, they cannot remain viable over time. However, if businesses combine the two (cost management and value creation), then they create a self-sustaining system that produces continuous growth. Businesses that successfully manage costs will protect their profits while also creating value in ways consumers understand and appreciate. The duality of cost management and value creation gives businesses resilience to remain in business and remain relevant to consumers.

Having competitive costs keeps you in the game, and having differentiated value enables you to win.

Balancing both competitive cost and differentiated value doesn't just represent a tag line. It serves as the foundation for long-term success. Keeping your prices competitive prevents you from being priced out of the marketplace.

Ensuring that your customers remember you requires differentiated value. When both work together, it allows you to compete beyond just competing with others; it enables you to lead them. With the changing landscape of the Indian marketplace, a combined effort toward achieving both is no longer just a wish; it's a necessity. It will dictate whether a company becomes a price warrior, a value provider, or a true catalyst for market change.

The balance of cost competitiveness and value creation is best demonstrated by the Tata Ace (Chhota Hathi). Before launching, no other mini truck had offered such utility and affordability. In designing the Ace, the company took a different approach to provide a lightweight vehicle for last-mile transportation and to enable small and medium entrepreneurs to generate a reliable source of income. The company-maintained focus on controlling costs during development; however, the goal was to deliver a product that balanced cost and function/durability/utility. The result was a product that not only sold but also created jobs for many, allowed entrepreneurs to start and grow businesses, and transformed the market. Cost competitiveness and value creation can work together toward success.

Just as with the Nano, the Nexon EV also had to follow this exact path and ultimately found success because the company struck a balance as originators in the value proposition for end users. The pricing was equally competitive, and at the same time, they were able to encompass so much more through the design excellence they incorporated into the vehicle, as well as the robustness of the safety features, all of which combined to create an aspirational product for the customers.

With the Nexon EV, it has been proven that there is a place in India for electric vehicles to provide both accessibility and desirability; the car established itself as a choice rather than a compromise.

This also showed that value can be a differentiator when the cost is being managed purposefully.

An example of how cost and value can complement one another is the electric bus subscription model, which allows cities to leapfrog from diesel to EV without incurring capital costs. The OEM/operator consortium procures buses, invests in charging infrastructure, manages maintenance & uptime, and bears technology and battery risks; the transport authority pays only for service delivered and avoids heavy upfront capital expenditure. The pricing is competitive, but it has provided the commuter and the city administrator with more value and the potential for much greater savings. This is a clear demonstration of a business model that creates both greater value and greater affordability. The concept is consistent across all of these examples: By integrating disciplined cost management and thoughtful design, understanding the customer, and applying technological insight, we multiply our ability to create value. This interrelationship, where cost effectiveness and value can work synergistically, is the only area in which we will develop true competitive advantage, not by choosing between cost and value, but by mastering both.

When an organization uses both cost and value as tools, it is no longer on the defensive but is instead establishing the rules of competition. Therein lies the true value advantage; there is no compromise. By using both cost and value as assets, we unlock value, create opportunities for innovation, and create organizations that earn the respect of our customers and make it exceedingly hard for our competitors to recreate. Admittedly, as I reflect on a couple of decades in industry, one thing is abundantly clear: companies that equated cost leadership with competitiveness paid the price. Companies that embraced cost discipline, however, found that locating differentiated value-built resilience, relevance, and leadership.

Lessons from Failures	Lessons from Successes
In the past, the **Nokia** brand was considered the world's most reliable mobile phone manufacturer. However, Nokia had a narrow focus on short-term profitability, prioritizing operating margins, production efficiencies, and customer needs, and forgetting to evolve with the times as smartphone technology emerged. As a result, Nokia has lost relevance in the current mobile phone marketplace.	Tata Motors' turnaround was not driven solely by cost reduction. Cost competitiveness was only one lever within a broader transformation agenda. Structural changes were made to improve organizational responsiveness to shifting market conditions, while waste was systematically identified, eliminated, and reinvested through stronger processes. These gains were intentionally channeled into product innovation and design to enhance customer-centricity rather than weaken capability. Initiatives such as the Ace mini truck, the Nexon EV, and the electric bus platform were developed to deliver competitive pricing, create differentiated customer value, restore market confidence, and establish a resilient foundation for long-term growth.
Kodak had the technology to produce digital images, yet the company was hesitant to invest in this area because of its focus on protecting its film revenue margins. In its pursuit of aggressive cost containment, Kodak failed to recognize the price-to-value relationship	The **Apple** case study shows how a disciplined approach to cost management can deliver exceptional customer value. The discipline of establishing an efficient supply chain through economies of scale allows Apple to protect its profit margins, and it has built brand loyalty through its

customers sought. As a result, the brand, which once **dominated this industry segment, soon became non-existent**.	innovative design and technology. Apple is a perfect example of how a focus on cost management and premium product positioning can exist in a complementary fashion.
Jet Airways and **Kingfisher Airlines** exemplify how cutting costs without addressing core operational issues can lead to catastrophic results for an airline. Jet Airways' aggressive cost-cutting to boost margins led to a significant decline in service quality and a loss of customer trust. Kingfisher has dazzled consumers with its style and glamour, yet failed to achieve a sustainable price-to-value balance, resulting in a mountain of debt that ultimately led to the company's bankruptcy.	**Unilever** uses its headquarters in India as its global base to demonstrate how to create efficiencies globally and operate in close concert with how consumers want to purchase. Unilever demonstrates an impressive ability to be cost-effective, maintain high-quality standards, and remain a relevant player across many markets worldwide.
Satyam Computers has become a classic example of the risks of being too focused on cost management rather than on building lasting, sustainable value. While Satyam's downfall involved multiple aspects of business operations, its inability to marry integrity, innovation, and cost management has created a permanent loss of trust for the company.	**Infosys,** by delivering cost-effective services through world-class processes and innovation, created a business model that changed how the world sees Indian IT and enabled it to compete on the global stage, based not only on cost but also on trust and quality.

The failures show what happens when low costs are the driving force behind a company's agenda, with no innovation, reinvestment, or direct consumer focus. The failures illustrate a company that pursued high margins and rapid growth through shortcuts, ultimately becoming irrelevant or failing altogether.

Conversely, the successes demonstrate that when a company successfully combines low cost with differentiated value, the result is excellent: resilience, customer loyalty, and long-term growth.

Asian Paints has no failures; therefore, it stands alone. Asian Paints' example shows that by instituting efficiency and value creation within an organization, a company can circumvent the traps that other companies have fallen into. The juxtaposition of the two groups illustrates that business leaders must be adept at both cost and value creation to avoid repeating past mistakes in their respective industries.

What Leaders Must Do Differently

The issue the companies with negative returns faced was cutting costs, albeit without innovation, reinvestment, or a fundamental understanding of their customers. They did not think strategically, only reacted tactically.

There is a simple answer, in principle, yet challenging work in practice:

- Think long-term. Business is a marathon, not a sprint.
- Reinvest savings. Channel efficiencies into innovation, capability building, and customer-centric improvements.
- Balance cost and value. Never sacrifice one for the other; let each reinforce the other.
- Listen to the customer. Ultimately, the customer is the ultimate judge of whether cost decisions create or erode value.

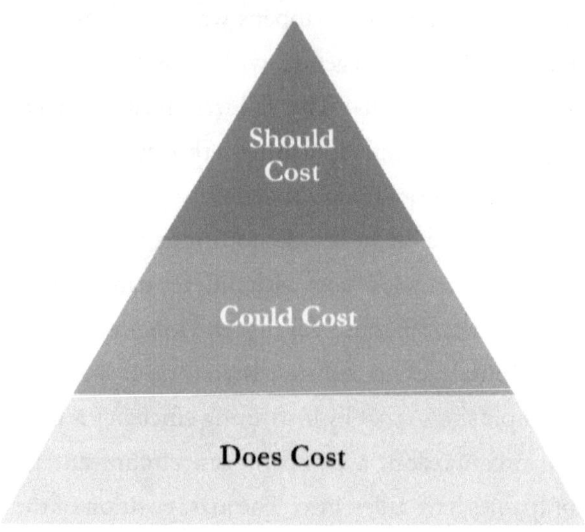

The Three Cost Views

Competitive cost builds resilience, while differentiated value builds relevance. Together, they create sustainable advantage. Leaders who embrace this principle will avoid the traps of the past and shape companies that endure.

Over time, I have come to rely on a simple framework to test whether cost reduction is truly strategic:

Many companies focus only on a product's price (i.e., "does cost" or "could cost") and make minor incremental improvements. Companies wishing to maintain their competitiveness must focus on understanding their operations and on eliminating as much waste as possible, while still providing and/or enhancing value. Value Engineering does not necessarily mean doing things as inexpensively as possible; it is about redesigning processes, materials, and/or products to maximize benefits while reducing overall costs.

Whenever I evaluate a cost decision, I ask myself one question: Does this reduction enhance or erode customer value? If it erodes value, it is not sustainable. If it enhances value, then the cost decision builds long-term advantage.

Every leader should remember what I call the value creation trilogy: growth, profitability, and cash. Growth keeps the organization relevant, profitability ensures viability, and cash secures the flexibility to invest in the future. If any one of these three is ignored, competitiveness suffers.

Strategic cost management, therefore, is not an isolated exercise. It is the discipline of aligning costs with value, asking the right questions, and balancing the three key elements. When leaders apply this mindset, they turn cost from a pressure point into a powerful driver of sustained value.

Audit Your Decisions and Make Sure You're Applying Your Decisions

Let's do something powerful together: let's do an easy exercise. Take a step back and think about the last three cost-related decisions your business made. These can be cost cuts, such as supplier negotiations, layoffs, or material changes (new), or process changes. Now think about it again through the "value-retained" lens on each of these decisions, or apply the value-retained principle to each of these cost-related decisions.

The main question you should be asking is: When my organization made these cost-related decisions, did it retain value for the client, erode it, improve the efficiency of the process without affecting the client's trust in my organization, or was it simply all about saving my organization money at the expense of loyalty? The answer to these questions will not be an academic exercise.

Still, it will be an efficient exercise that will tell you how well you are doing as a business, and you will be able to use the results of this exercise to improve those aspects of your business if they are failing. I developed what I call a three-step decision test.

The problem we see in so many organizations today is that they equate urgency with effective decision-making and chase numbers at the expense of building and maintaining a competitive position. The issue isn't cutting costs; it's cutting costs without considering value. As a result, employees become disengaged, customers leave, and once-strong brands become unviable.

Simultaneously, the contrary is equally valid. Every time I have witnessed leaders address cost with precision, I have seen organizations flourish. Waste is eradicated without sacrificing value, savings are reinvested in innovation, and the customer experience and competitiveness transition from tenuous to sustainable.

For that reason, I do not consider the cost–value paradox to be something to avoid, but an opportunity to embrace. For leaders who are willing to reconsider, the paradox provides them with their own capital. It compels us to stop treating cost and value as adversaries, and to begin managing them as allies.

The reason this is harder than it sounds lies in what I call the cost–value paradox. Cost is visible, measurable, and immediate. Value, on the other hand, is subtle, future-oriented, and often uncertain. Organizations, therefore, tend to cut what they can measure and lose what they cannot yet see.

This paradox becomes especially dangerous when investments in innovation, digital capabilities, or ESG are framed purely as costs rather than as investments in future value. The damage does not occur because the organization spent more today, but because it quietly protected less of tomorrow. Over time, competitiveness erodes, not through reckless decisions, but through perfectly rational ones made with an incomplete view of value.

Chapter 2
Building a Precision Mindset

While I often think of the company I referenced before that cut its costs significantly to the point where its Market share disappeared completely, it at first glance seems like an example of wasteful cutting to the extreme. Upon further examination, however, it is clear that their main issue was not the practice of cutting costs at all, but the lack of precision in doing so.

The company in question operated with a lack of clarity about the cuts; acted out of alignment with its true purpose, vision, and goals; and executed with little to no consistency across departments. They conflated activity with progress, which is a common pitfall for many leaders today.

They assume that saving money makes them immediately more competitive, but that's not true. If a company focuses exclusively on reducing costs, it may become leaner, but it will lack the ability to strategically position itself for success in the marketplace. A company must not only be lean, but also lean on purpose. This means they must have a clear understanding of how making efficient use of their resources (efficiency) can support increased value, and, conversely, when inefficient use of resources may jeopardize value. I call the latter the distinction of precision. Precision allows you to differentiate a shortcut approach to cutting costs versus a sustainable long-term solution. However, precision is not perfection. Perfection may delay action, but precision accelerates outcomes. This will be dealt with in further detail in this chapter.

When precision in cost decision-making is lacking, cost-related activities are implemented in your organization as blunt-force trauma, creating distrust, eroding quality, and disengaging employees. When you have precision, you use efficiency to strengthen your company, create a targeted approach that leverages your cost discipline, streamline processes to avoid redundancy, and ensure that your customers never feel your company has compromised quality.

I have seen evidence of this across industries. Some organizations only get there more quickly, often, without precision, which leads them to go in circles. Then, some organizations create with discipline and clarity, producing more for less, even in the face of uncertainty. The difference is not that they cut more unsuccessfully; instead, they think more precisely.

In developing the mindset this chapter focuses on, precision is not perfection, nor is it being pedantic about every detail taken into account when making decisions. Instead, precision is the clearness with which one makes decisions, the consistency with which one delivers on them, and the purposefulness with which one operates. Thus, when an organization's cost competitiveness and value-added activities align, it no longer has to choose between survival and growth; it can do both simultaneously.

From my own experience, precision is the supporting connective tissue that links cost competitiveness with value; cost competitiveness alone does not guarantee long-term sustained competitive advantage, while value creation without the discipline of operating with precision will soon become unsustainable. However, when linking the two through the concept of precision, the organization operates in a new learning rhythm that enables it to operate with maximum efficiency without compromising the value it creates for customers, while allowing it to grow more rapidly without creating waste.

This is more evident in R&D expenses when an organization develops modular platforms rather than one-off designs. That reduces the number of product variants and lowers development costs per model, and similarly, for digital simulation before physical prototyping, when more CAE (Computer Aided Engineering) is used. CFD (Computational Fluid Dynamics) and digital twins are used to validate a significant percentage of performance virtually, enabling fewer prototypes and faster cycles.

Consider the precision of the synergistic relationship between clarity and consistency. It makes it clear where costs may be reduced, where processes may be streamlined, and what impact those decisions may have on the customer. It is the consistency of performance, such that what is promised is delivered every time, in every interaction. With fewer surprises, fewer contradictions, and fewer wasted resources due to misalignment, precision enables smoother operations.

Leadership confusion often stems from conflating two very similar ideas: being prepared for any situation and the pursuit of perfection in everything that we do. Perfectionism, at its core, is the continued effort to ensure the decisions we make and the steps we take toward success are as perfect as possible. With this mindset, perfectionists will continue to spend the necessary time and resources pursuing the unattainable promise of perfection. When pursuing an idealistic vision of success, businesses are often forced to deal with frustration and hindered growth.

On the other hand, leaders can create certainty around their decisions by relying on factual data and evidence, and aligning their thought processes, allowing them to confidently create a course of action without falling prey to the pitfalls of analysis paralysis. In addition, they can instill confidence in their ability to accurately assess risk, resulting in data essentially equivalent to that of the perfectionist leader.

As a result, businesses that make cost decisions based on precision eliminate the uncertainty of guessing what costs will be. Instead, they can use their precision to develop a strategy to optimize the company's resource investment.

Additionally, by using precision to define growth potential, businesses now have access to a scalable growth model. In both cases, the multiplier effect of using precision creates an opportunity for further growth as other companies leverage these competencies.

Precision is about more than just the operational aspect of a business. It serves as the bridge that connects efficiency to action, value to cost. As a result, businesses must create a measurable balance between the two extremes noted above to maintain long-term competitiveness.

Precision in Business

People often treat precision as though it were synonymous with accuracy. When we speak of accuracy, we refer to a level of correctness; when we speak of precision, we refer to a higher level of significance. In the business context, this means exhibiting clarity in decision-making processes and consistency in executing business operations.

A measure of accuracy can still lead to an imprecise direction. A sales forecast, for example, may be accurate in its numbers but not accurate in its guidance to action. Precision ensures that decisions are both factually correct and actionable, aligned, and sustainable. It requires us to articulate not only what is to be done, but how it is to be done and why that is meaningful.

In my experience, I have witnessed firsthand how a lack of precision results in significant time waste.

Teams are pulled in multiple directions, departmental objectives are determined by what is convenient for each department, and resources are consumed, resulting in little to no actual results.

The practice of precision, therefore, cultivates a culture of definitive priority throughout a company, aligning management and employees on execution goals and enabling managers to make the best possible use of their hours, money, and decision-making ability.

Precision or Perfectionism

There is often a misunderstanding between precision and perfectionism. Perfectionism is the belief that everything should be perfect right off the bat. Perfectionism creates a fear of failure; nothing gets done when you pursue perfection. I have witnessed companies where leaders paralyzed their employees because they wanted a "perfect plan." By the time that perfect plan was developed, the opportunity had expired. Precision is the opposite, enabling employees to take action with confidence.

While a precise decision is not the same as a perfect decision, it provides clarity and consistency about how an action aligns with values. Precision is selecting the best decision based on the information available to you and executing that decision with precision. Precision does not involve taking unnecessary risks, nor does it involve unnecessary second-guessing or overthinking.

Perfectionism delays taking action. By contrast, precision provides the basis for taking productive action.

The company developed a broad-based Budget with projected sales figures and cost estimates. It could experience a significant decline in margins. This is a lack of precision when a top-down budgeting process needs to be reconciled with bottom-up, granular budgeting, and when the right target setting at the right time is required, supported by a robust governance mechanism.

With granular, product-wise P&L analysis, which analyzes profitability at the individual product or process level rather than the segment level, the root cause of the problem and the required action are understood. While some product lines appeared profitable at the high level, upon examination of their actual costs, it became clear that they were actually losing money. At the same time, other products or processes that were not given a second glance were the key drivers for EBITDA.

By shifting from broad budgeting to granular, precision-based profit-and-loss statements (P&Ls), the company could identify where waste was hidden and where investment was overdue. Within a short time, EBITDA could improve significantly, not because of a new product launch or a market shift, but simply because precision brought visibility, alignment, and consistency to their cost and value management.

The Precision Equation

Precision equals Visibility multiplied by Alignment and Consistency.

- **Visibility**: Do you see the proper drivers of cost and value, or are they hidden under averages and assumptions?
- **Alignment**: Are your decisions and actions pulling in the same direction across departments, or working at cross purposes?
- **Consistency**: Can you execute decisions reliably, so customers and stakeholders experience the same quality every time?

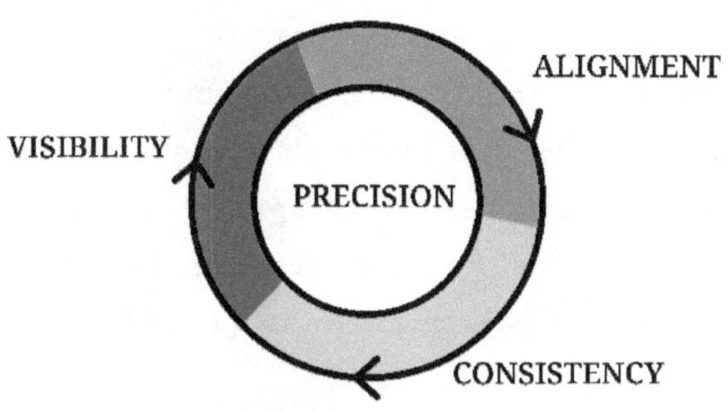

Pecision = Visibility x Alignment x Consistency

When all three are present, precision takes root. When even one is missing, waste, confusion, and inefficiency creep in.

Precision is not just about achieving an accurate number; defined precision means ensuring clarity, consistency, and reliability for the organization.

There is almost always a meaningful cost saving and longer-term value creation associated with precision. Organizations without precision act like ships set adrift with the tide.

The precision compasses will align the ship and head it toward growth.

Precision is the outcome of clear visibility, strategic alignment, and disciplined consistency. Visibility shows reality, alignment sets direction, consistency delivers precision.

Eliminating Misalignment

Misalignment between departments results in high hidden costs for organizations. Typically, each department will define its own success, priorities, and measurements. For instance, sales focus on driving volume, while operations manage costs; finance aims for margins; and marketing works to establish brand equity. Due to the emphasis on specific departmental goals, a significant number of cases will arise in which the actions taken conflict with one another.

I have seen many organizations lose millions of dollars to misalignment between departments stemming from operating independently rather than from poor strategy or a lack of talented resources. I have seen cases in which production capacity was booked without verifying the production schedule, and promotions were executed over the holiday period without considering the impact of distribution costs.

For example, finance assumed it had the authority to implement cuts, but those cuts led to reduced service levels and, ultimately, a loss of clients.

Every department was "accurate" in establishing its own measure of success, but ultimately, the organization as a whole was not aligned.

The accuracy of decisiveness is what eliminates this leakage. When decisions are made with visibility, alignment, and consistency, then departments stop acting in silos. Every action aligns with common priorities, leading not only to less waste but also to a much more meaningful impact.

Identifying ROI Hotspots

Precision also enables profitable growth by identifying ROI hotspots, areas where small investments yield significant returns.

By contrast, without precision, companies distribute their resources widely, and their budgets are generally relatively even across departments or products. This seems fair on paper, but in reality, not all activities create the same value. Precision tells the truth.

I am aware of a situation in which the organization undertook rigorous profitability analysis of its product portfolio. To their surprise, they found that nearly 30 percent of their resources were expended on products that contributed less than 10 percent to profits.

At the same time, they had a small number of significant offerings with proven sales track records that were underfunded.

By targeting the resources to improve returns on investment, the team achieved improved revenue and margins without increasing net investment. This is where precision creates a multiplier effect. It not only cuts waste but also unlocks growth by channeling resources into the right places.

Scaling with Lower Waste

Growth is often assumed to require higher overheads, more staff, bigger systems, and more processes. However, I have observed that when growth is driven by precision, overhead need not increase at the same rate. Precision enables businesses to scale intelligently. Clear priorities eliminate redundancies. Data-informed insights maximize efficiency along the way. Consistency of approach mitigates costly rework. Precision cuts through scaling complexity rather than adding more complexity.

The distinction can be especially pronounced in rapidly scaling domains, such as logistics. For businesses that grow without precision, delays, complaints, and costs can escalate quickly. Conversely, a business that becomes a champion of precision can scale with confidence, adding customers and volume without sacrificing efficiency.

I recall a situation in which a logistics company faced this very dilemma. They were scaling fast but were beginning to experience late deliveries from their teams, higher fuel costs, and lower margins. While, at first glance, adding drivers and vehicles seemed like the answer to increased delivery demand, this would only increase overhead costs.

Instead, they turned to precision. They used the GPS data they had and advanced routing optimization tools available to analyze delivery patterns in detail. They recognized that many delays and increased fuel consumption were due to poor routing and unnecessary idle time. By redesigning routes with precision, they reduced fuel costs by double digits, cut delivery times, and significantly improved on-time performance. What's more, they achieved this without expanding their fleet. Growth continued, but waste was removed, not added.

This is the power of precision: the company becomes more competitive, more reliable, and more profitable by seeing clearly and acting consistently.

Precision turns the subject of cost containment into an opportunity to facilitate growth without excess baggage. By eliminating misalignment, focusing on the higher-ROI spots, and reducing waste, precision can become a multiplier of productivity. The logistics example is just one; the principle applies everywhere. Precision does not slow growth; it makes growth more profitable.

Precision Powers Value

One of the most significant benefits of precision is that it forces clarity of priorities. I have seen many organizations attempt to do everything at once, multiple projects, endless initiatives, and a scattered focus. The result is that resources get diluted, and customers rarely feel the impact.

When there is ambiguity about priorities, the budget is tight, talent is underutilized, and decision-making is reactive. Precision takes care of all of that. It requires leaders to ask, which activities really matter? Which projects impact customer outcomes? As soon as these two questions become clear, leaders can allocate resources more effectively and have a greater impact on customers. In my own journey, the companies that stand out are not necessarily those with the most significant budgets, but rather those with the clearest priorities. Precision channels energy where it matters most, ensuring that every rupee spent, every hour worked, and every idea developed delivers meaningful value. Establishing value is about first quantifying it. Many business leaders define value in terms of satisfaction, loyalty, and engagement, but these are generally broad, conceptual terms that may not fully capture the essence of customer value.

Precision provides a means for the conversation around customer value to become more disciplined and objective, as it ties the concept directly to the measurable outcomes it delivers. Rather than using vanity metrics as the basis for this measure, precision provides a more objective view of the cost to the organization of producing each unit of customer value. This value "unit" can take on different definitions, ranging from on-time delivery of product to resolution of service issues, to successful delivery of product features, to even measurable changes in customer sentiment.

An example of this shift in the customer value discussion comes from one of my previous experiences with a digital transformation leader; as he stated, "We stopped asking how much our products cost per unit to produce, and started asking how much it costs to produce an impact?" That single shift in thinking changed how an organization assessed its own performance. By defining customer value in terms of measurable metrics, the organization was able to identify precisely how much value was generated for its customers through the expense it incurred, as well as where the expense generated activity without generating value for customers; this enabled more precise decision-making, improved alignment of teams, and a significantly more strategic decision-making approach regarding allocation of effort/investment.

The Precision within your system/organization also plays a role in the second principal value of "Trust". Customers do not come back to you because you provided them a single "Positive" experience with your product. They return because they have confidence that they will continue to have "Positive" experiences with your product every time they purchase it. While Brand Slogans/Brand Campaigns might create "Trust" for a short period of time, "Trust" must be earned over time by providing flawless, predictable, and repeatable execution of your products and services.

As long as every component of your system operates as intended, the level of quality remains consistent across all service interactions, and the expectations of your customers are consistently met, the customer will see the value of your Precision, even if they cannot articulate their experience. As a result, customers have confidence that their experience will be the same every time, thereby creating the "Trust" component of your brand's overall value. The ability to build "Trust" is critical in a business environment where customers have limitless choices and very little time.

Therefore, not only does Precision reduce the likelihood of making "Mistakes" in product or service delivery, but it also builds confidence in the brand/company. Confidence is one of the most essential forms of "Value" an organization can offer/create, and the sustainability of customer confidence will lead to massive brand or company Equity for your organization.

I recall a leadership team that was struggling with R&D costs. Projects were overrunning budgets, new features were being developed without apparent customer demand, and overall spending was rising without visible returns.

A precision-driven approach was introduced by analyzing customer usage analytics in depth. Instead of assuming what customers wanted, the team looked at actual behavior data: which features were used most, which were ignored, and which gaps customers complained about.

The figures showed that more than a quarter of the continuing research and development funding went into developing options that customers seldom used. By aligning their product development priorities with measurable analytics, the company could reduce R&D expenditure and increase customer satisfaction by focusing on developing what consumers were genuinely interested in purchasing.

This situation could not have been identified as a reduction in R&D; instead, it was identified as a reduction in R&D waste and an amplification of R&D's positive contribution. Through precise analytics, it was determined that the conversation shifted from "What are our current expenses for R&D?" to "What is the economic benefit created by R&D?" The effect of precision on value is that organizations can move their focus from doing things to producing outcomes. Once organizations have accurate priorities defined, their efforts are concentrated on these identified areas; when outcomes are created based on the organization's objectives, they invest in those areas; and when organizations are steadfast in delivering reliable outcomes, they build credibility with customers. Customers will recognize and reward this credibility through loyalty and continued patronage. That is what the true power of precision represents: cost-effectiveness and measurable value.

Tools & Practices for Precision

Precision is not merely a mindset, but a discipline supported by tools and practices. Throughout my career, I have seen the incredible benefits that leaders can realize when they help their organizations establish the right systems for clarity, alignment, and consistency. Precision does not happen by chance; it is accomplished through data, routines, and technology.

The first stage of Precision is to make data-driven decisions rather than rely on gut feelings. I have always considered using analytics, dashboards, and granular product profit-and-loss (P&L) statements for precision.

The benefit of having a granular product P&L is that it helps leaders better understand where their profits are being earned and where they are being siphoned away.

Dashboards enhance this knowledge by providing real-time visibility of the most current indicators, rather than those reported at the end of the prior quarter. A well-designed dashboard shows more than just total sales; it highlights conversion rates, order fulfilment timeframes, complaints resolved, and even cost per impact. By consistently using this type of information to make decisions, leaders can shift their perspective from reactive to proactive, taking appropriate actions based on the evidence. Precision follows suit.

Data alone cannot ensure precision. Teams need to continuously realign through strong feedback loops to refine and calibrate team performance over time. As a benchmark for alignment, I have focused on creating regularly scheduled rituals—daily standup meetings, retrospectives, and structured review meetings—to identify problems that might escalate or create other issues during the development process. Customer feedback loops are also critical, and annual surveys are too slow and narrow. For leaders to succeed, they must have real-time visibility into customer usage patterns, service interactions, and social media activity. Therefore, leaders can quickly, accurately, and confidently adjust their priorities when they have continuous access to feedback loops.

Continuous feedback loops will keep organizations grounded, keep their focus on value creation, and prevent organizations from drifting away from their corporate objectives.

The use of technology has dramatically expanded the possibilities for making predictions. AI, automation, and predictive analytics are now everyday tools that allow for greater accuracy than was previously available, through the use of artificial intelligence to find the patterns in large amounts of data that human beings would have difficulty finding, through automation to remove human errors associated with repetitive manual tasks and through predictive analytics to provide managers with warning of potential problems in relation to the health of equipment, the stability of supply chains, and the retention of customers. Predictive maintenance has been shown to decrease downtime of the equipment resulting in a reduction in costs for both the company and its customers, while AI driven predictive demand forecasting has allowed many organizations to produce and maintain their inventory at levels that better reflect demand which results in fewer stockouts, reduced inventory holding costs, and delighted customers as a result of using technology for good.

For precision to be achieved continuously and become the norm in the workplace, it must be underpinned by three pillars: data for clarity, feedback loops for alignment, and technology for consistency at scale. When these three elements work together, they enable precision in an operational business, not just as an aspiration.

Embedding Precision as Culture

Precision must not just be a tool or a project; it must become part of an organization's culture. I have seen organizations that spent money on analytics tools or dashboards, only to see little to no change as a result.

The reason is that precision was never established about how we, as an organization, would operate. If we are going to continue to use Precision as a way of working, it has to be treated as a collective discipline. It must be threaded throughout the organization by Leadership, Daily Rituals, and Language.

Leadership aligns with the concept of precision: when leaders share a vision, language, and priorities, they create clarity and alignment within the organization. Leadership that is unclear and inconsistent leads to misinterpretation and misalignment.

For leaders to align with the model's success, they must agree on a common language, establish measurable goals, and use precision in decision-making to achieve the most effective results. When leaders exhibit precision, those they lead will instinctively do the same.

Rituals such as daily huddles, weekly reviews, and retrospective meetings foster rhythm within an organization. These habits provide a cadence for teams to maintain focus on results, stay aligned, and prevent drifting apart. Key Performance Indicators (KPIs) should be established for each team so that all members understand them and use them in their decision-making. When KPIs and self-reviews are clear and shared, the concept of precision becomes an everyday practice, stabilizing the organization and building trust based on data and facts, rather than moods.

The use of precise language also enhances precision. Using vague instructions such as "Do it soon" or "Make it better" can lead to misinterpretations. Providing clear definitions of the terms will eliminate confusion, reduce the need to redo tasks, and increase confidence. For example, if you were to say "by Friday at 5:00 PM" instead of "soon," or "Reduce defects by 10%" instead of "Make it better," it would eliminate confusion, reduce the need to redo work, and increase confidence.

In my experience, I once worked with a team of leaders who struggled to decide on product development priorities. The meetings consisted of lots of debates from everyone; however, the arguments were all ambiguous, such as "This product is essential," "This feature is sure to be popular," or "We must get this done faster." Everyone had an opinion, but no one demonstrated accuracy.

We altered the dialogue by incorporating actual metrics based on the features customers actually used. The conversation was no longer about beliefs, but about facts: which features customers used most, which they did not even consider using, and the gap. This clarity changed the roadmap.

We stopped building low-value features and allocated developers to high-value feature areas. We saved time and money while developing products that customers really wanted and needed.

That experience reinforced my belief: precision in culture begins with leaders, is sustained through rituals, and is reinforced in language. When these three come together, precision becomes a way of life.

Avoiding the Pitfalls

While precision is a powerful enabler of growth and competitiveness, I have also seen how easily it can be misunderstood or misapplied. When that happens, precision stops being a strength and turns into a trap. There are three pitfalls' leaders must guard against.

Incorrect use of precision can create "analysis paralysis," leading an organization to drown in a sea of information and delay vital business decisions. Instead of creating the clarity and confidence for leaders to make the best possible decisions faster, precision can, in some cases, cause leaders to become "paralyzed" and unable to act quickly due to overwhelming amounts of information.

Leaders need a clear understanding of how their business metrics relate to their customers, enabling them to make better decisions faster. If a leader focuses on the wrong metric, he creates a perception of success; in fact, he creates a perception of inefficiency.

Misuse of metrics can lead organizations to celebrate their efficiency while ignoring signs of declining value. For example, a company with low supply chain costs was thrilled to celebrate its success while ignoring the fact that it was experiencing significant increases in customer complaints.

By focusing on metrics that do not connect to outcome metrics, leaders can create a false sense of confidence while incurring high costs of value.

Many leaders believe that over-precision, or waiting indefinitely for perfect information to make decisions, is a form of procrastination. Therefore, leaders need sufficient clarity and speed to make timely, confident decisions. Top-performing organizations develop a framework for determining when they have reached the "sufficient precision" threshold, enabling them to take proactive action. Therefore, precision can be a significant strategic advantage when appropriately utilized; however, it can also hinder an organization's speed and success when used poorly.

Precision is a growth driver, not just an efficiency discipline, based on my own professional experiences. Most leaders typically see Precision as a tool to eliminate waste or establish stronger controls, which is true, but it does not capture all that Precision truly represents. Ultimately, the real value of Precision to an organization is that it helps accelerate growth, enable more intelligent scaling, and deliver value with greater reliability.

Organizations measuring their costs or value created should shift from traditional cost-per-unit metrics (i.e., the cost to produce one widget, complete one transaction, or make one delivery) to a more meaningful metric: cost-per-impact (i.e., the cost of creating one unit of customer value). For example, let's talk about on-time deliveries, resolved service issues, or actual customer use of features. These metrics demonstrate the importance of focusing on creating value for the customer rather than producing output for the organization.

Every organization ultimately strives to build trust by delivering consistent results. By clearly defining priorities, consistently following through, and communicating transparently with customers and employees about organizational metrics, organizations can be very confident that their customers will receive the highest level of service and the least wasted resources possible.

As a result, an organization's actions can grow without requiring additional support or overhead costs. Ultimately, this translates into an organization's ability to deliver consistent value to its customers and establish a competitive advantage in the market.

I have seen organizations change their approach as they transition precision from simply an accounting process to a leadership discipline. Precision will save you dollars and, in turn, create value. Precision will limit waste and, in turn, create resilience. Precision will support better operations and, in turn, create pathways to sustainable growth. To the leaders out there, the bottom line is simple: when you develop precision into your culture, decision-making, and metrics, you will find a competitive advantage that extends far beyond efficiency.

I suggest a challenge that can significantly illuminate how your organization really operates. Think back on the last three major decisions made in your company. Examples include pricing decisions, hiring decisions, product launches, supplier contracts, or decision-making processes that significantly impact outcomes. Try to consider this with sober judgment, and ask these questions:

- Did we base our decisions on facts, and was the data accurate, or were they essentially assumptions?
- Did we have views of what the actual costs or impact were, or were we working from averages and gut feelings?
- Were all departments aligned, or did each department interpret the information differently?

It's a straightforward exercise that might reveal some startling information. It will show whether you have precision integrated into your decision-making process, or if you are overly reliant on instinct and shortcuts. After that, locate one portion of your business where you could immediately improve profitability based on outputs by applying greater precision without adding additional expense. It might be something as sophisticated as optimizing supply chain routing, or as basic as how you allocate R&D or measure customer satisfaction. Precision often reveals that the actual opportunity is not to do more, but to do what you already do with more clarity, consistency, and alignment.

Ultimately, consider this question: Where is precision creating savings and growth today? The answer will not be the same for every organization, but the principle will remain the same everywhere. Precision creates visibility, which enables more informed decisions. It brings teams together and reduces waste. It enables consistency and encourages trust.

The message is clear: do not wait for a crisis to adopt precision. Start now. Assess, determine, and act.

You will reap rewards not only in lower costs but also in increased growth and deeper customer loyalty.

The lessons learned from examining the companies that lost market share and were forced to cut costs have consistently been the same: cutting costs did not kill them; it was their lack of precision. These companies made cost reductions without a clear purpose, acted without all departments being aligned, and executed plans without ensuring consistency across departments. As such, they were not competitive; instead, they fell apart.

This is why precision is much more than just a skill for managers; it is an entire way of looking at business opportunities.

When leaders utilize precision as a lens to view their business, they can identify activity vs. impact and align every rupee, hour, and project with actual value to their customers. By using precision, leaders can shorten their time-to-market without creating unnecessary delays, scale their efforts without wasting resources, and develop innovative solutions without losing control.

In addition to having clarity of vision and understanding how to leverage precision, one also needs a firm foundation to connect the various decision points throughout the business. The original example illustrates how failure to use precision has ruined many companies; conversely, the opportunity for your success lies in this principle and in leveraging it within a strong framework to ensure every decision creates multiplier effects on value. Precision is not a skill; it is a culture where assumptions are challenged, details matter, and 'almost' is never enough. Organizations transform faster when precision guides judgement, not just measurement. Decision-making becomes powerful the moment precision replaces approximation, because clarity always costs less than confusion.

Chapter 3
Frameworks for Strategic Cost Competitiveness

At a recent leadership meeting, five senior managers gathered to discuss a possible cost-cutting strategy. They were all armed with their own spreadsheets, each cell filled with color and each number defended as though it were a core value. After two hours of discussion, an overwhelming number of formulas had been created with no clear outcome. The meeting concluded that everyone had "optimized" their cost-cutting strategy. Still, there was no clear explanation of which numbers actually improved customer satisfaction, strengthened the company's products, or ensured the organization's long-term viability.

This meeting taught me a vital lesson: if you cannot articulate your cost reduction strategy in five minutes or less with only a whiteboard in front of you, then you do not have a proper strategy, only a spreadsheet.

I see this same pattern across industries and sectors. When times get tough for companies, the first thing their leaders do is reach for the closest lever – stop travelling, freeze hiring, delay maintenance – thinking that they are saving costs. In reality, these leaders are only treating symptoms, not fixing systems. In most cases, leaders lack a clear framework to guide their cost-reduction decisions. As a result, they make reactive, temporary, and piecemeal decisions that ultimately make their organization busier, rather than better.

Simplicity, on the other hand, brings power. When you can express your cost logic as a clear line connecting purpose, process, and performance, you begin to see which costs are investments and which are inefficiencies. You begin to distinguish between what drives value and what merely consumes resources.

We previously discussed how precision enables clarity in an individual decision. Structure provides direction for the complete organization. Structure transforms cost control from an accounting exercise to a leadership discipline. Structure ensures that every rupee saved matters, reinvests the saved costs, and steers the enterprise toward long-term competitiveness.

This chapter focuses on developing a strategic framework that integrates individual and fragmented cost actions into a comprehensive, value-driven, and forward-looking system. Frameworks do not complicate decisions; they simplify them. Frameworks transition from bringing chaos to clarity, from spreadsheets to strategies.

Over time, I have come to understand that most organizations fail not because of a lack of data, but because of a lack of structure. When cost management is performed without a framework, it ceases to be a discipline of intentionality and becomes a contest of numbers. Individuals focus on controlling expenses rather than on strategic advancement. That is where the real opportunity is lost.

Cost competitiveness does not equate to lower spending. It is about the right spending. Cost, value, operations, and culture are entwined into a single source of energy that strives toward a common purpose. When these elements are connected, the journey toward cost decisions aligns with the customer outcomes, innovation, and sustainable profitability the organization seeks to achieve. When these elements are not connected and become transient in value creation, managing costs can become an exercise directly in conflict with the value the organization is creating.

Due to its structure, traditional budgeting is primarily reactive and led by the finance team. It provides direction on how much should be spent and where to make reductions, but does not generally include the reasons for those actions. Traditional budgeting primarily reflects historical outcomes rather than forecasting for future periods. Strategic frameworks, on the other hand, are developed into an enterprise-wide concept, so that all areas, such as design, sourcing, manufacturing, marketing, and service, can understand and evaluate how their actions will affect both costs and customer value.

The overall movement from control to intelligence will be the basis of strategic cost competitiveness. When leaders begin to adopt this approach, they will no longer ask themselves, "Where can we cut?" Instead, they will start to ask, "Where can we invest to create the most value per rupee?" This is the process of transformation.

The Need for a Strategic Framework

A significant number of organizations struggle to distinguish between activity and progress; therefore, executive leaders tend to respond to the pressures of quarterly reporting with quick, reactive actions such as travel bans, hiring freezes, contract renegotiations, or cost-cutting measures. While these actions can temporarily alleviate a sense of control- particularly when quarterly results are at stake- they do little to improve an organization's long-term competitiveness. Without a structure in place, the organization's cost-based actions become tactical and, more often than not, unrelated to the organization's long-term strategy. The danger of merely saving money is that a company lacks a unified system for creating value from its resources, as it views costs individually rather than in combination to develop value-based outcomes. Competitiveness requires that an organization design an integrated framework to systematically connect its cost decisions across different time horizons, functions, and outcomes.

Michael Porter's definition of strategy states that "the essence of strategy is making choices." Unstructured, cost-based decisions violate Porter's definition of strategy and result in confusion rather than clarity. A good strategic framework will assist organizational leaders in determining which costs are reasonable to retain to protect value and which are unreasonable (i.e., bad costs) because they create excessive or unnecessary levels of complexity. It will show the organization where to reduce costs and where not to; it emphasizes that an organization should exercise fiscal discipline before deciding on cost reductions.

The "finance fallacy" mistakenly assumes that the Finance Department is solely responsible for costs; however, costs are involved at every level of decision-making (e.g., Product Design, Sourcing, Operations, Customer Experience). This narrow approach will limit the decision space relevant to cost to financial decisions only, thereby creating a vacuum of potential information and limiting the ability to make informed decisions. For example, a reduction in overall costs may reduce Customer Experience by reducing Product Quality, whereas increasing volume without consideration of costs may negatively impact profit margins over time; therefore, a cross-functional solution must be developed for Finance, Design, Sourcing, Manufacturing, Marketing, and Customer Experience as a shared responsibility for developing products and services.

Quick wins are beneficial because they generate momentum and instill confidence, but they are only part of the solution if they fit within the overall cost-reduction framework.

A practical framework must ensure that the immediate impact of a Quick Win is balanced by its potential for improvement.

Efficiency in the Medium-Term and to transform the organization in the Long-Term, while maintaining a consistent cadence and preventing the organization from becoming complacent, cutting corners out of impatience, or burning out. This enables Organizational Agility during times when rapid action is required and Patience for planning during times when an extended timeline is warranted.

To illustrate my point, I often use a medical analogy: Imagine a patient who has recurring headaches. This person takes painkillers for headaches rather than learning what is causing them (e.g., Poor Vision, High Blood Pressure, etc.). Therefore, the pain may temporarily go away, but the underlying cause of the Headaches is still untreated. Therefore, this is similar to (reactive) Cutting Costs - it may relieve discomfort, but it does not cure the underlying "disease."

Leaders have used frameworks as diagnostic tools to better understand why an organization's inefficiencies occur and how to resolve them systematically; as a result, an organization can not only heal from its inefficiencies permanently but also heal at a structural level, rather than simply providing temporary solutions.

Additionally, the executive framework enables organizations to transition from reactive decision-making to reflective decision-making, from fragmented action to focused action, and from simply cutting costs to creating competitive advantage.

If executives want to build actual competitive cost advantages, this can only be realized through integrated systems of strategy and structure, Cost, purpose, and precision emanating from culture; this is why I have developed the Cost–Value Strategic Framework. A pyramid typically represents my model.

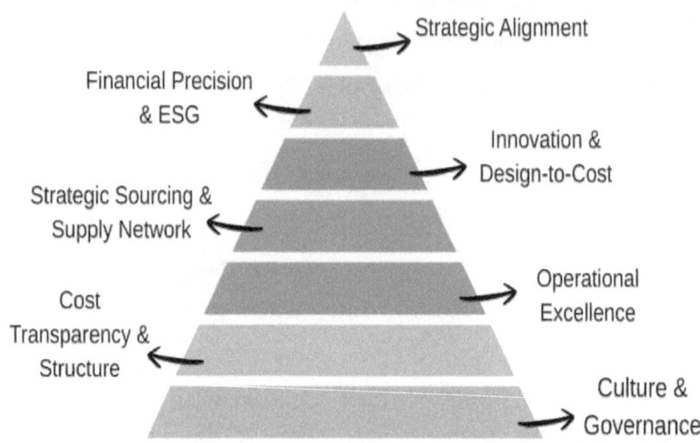

The Cost-Value Strategic Framework Pyramid

The base of the Strategic Cost Competitiveness Framework is Culture and Governance, which sets the foundation for accountability, decision-making, and organizational discipline. The next layer is Cost Transparency and Structure, represented by a single version of the truth across the enterprise, enabling clear and informed cost decisions. Above this is Operational Excellence, supported by Strategic Sourcing and Supply Network, which together drive efficiency, resilience, and value creation. The following layer includes Innovation and Design-to-Cost and Financial Precision and ESG, reinforcing disciplined investment, sustainability, and long-term competitiveness. At the top of the framework is Strategic Alignment, ensuring that all layers work together to achieve the organization's ultimate goals.

All layers of the Strategic Cost Competitiveness Framework support one another; therefore, cost decisions become not only efficient but also intelligent, ethical, and value-driven.

The foundation of the Strategic Cost Competitiveness Framework is Culture and Governance.

The Culture layer represents where the framework truly begins, as it provides the mental model for using the framework effectively.

Without a culture that supports the framework's objectives, no component of the framework can succeed in the long term. Organizations with advanced systems have failed simply because they lacked a culture of ownership. Culture creates the invisible infrastructure necessary to obtain cost competitiveness. Governance provides the primary structure that ensures the infrastructure of ownership and accountability will be consistent. When leaders model disciplined decision-making, transparency, and respect for shared values, the entire organization will automatically follow this example. Culture is the reason we make decisions; governance is how we sustain them. Together, Culture and Governance form the foundation of Strategic Cost Competitiveness.

Cost transparency and structure, two of the most powerful facilitators of alignment, are derived from this starting point. This "single version of truth," made available through transparency, provides a basis for honest discussions about performance without ambiguity. For example, when a manufacturing facility developed a "cost room" (a room filled with dashboards showing daily yield, scrap production, downtime, energy consumption, and the cost to produce an output), anyone from an operator to a senior executive at this facility could enter this room and understand how well their business was performing.

The information presented in the Cost Room was clearly visible, straightforward, and completely transparent. By seeing the same information as their peers, individuals could move from assigning blame to identifying and resolving issues and developing mutual trust. Operational excellence represents the next layer of capability.

Operational excellence represents the discipline of doing the right things every time without fail. Lean thinking, Kaizen, Poka Yoke, and related practices are just a few examples of continuous improvement critical to operational excellence. I have always been a proponent of the belief that operational excellence is less about making large-scale changes and more about making numerous small changes over time (small but consistent). Automation, scale efficiencies, and waste reduction not only provide cost savings but also create value. Every minute saved, each defect reduced, and each non-value-added activity eliminated adds to competitiveness and customer satisfaction.

The next layer above operational excellence is Strategic Sourcing and Supply Networks. Sourcing is more than simply buying things. Sourcing represents a company's strategy in motion. For the most resilient companies, suppliers are viewed as partners rather than vendors. The make-or-buy decision must be informed by long-term value versus short-term cost. Our experience during the pandemic has shown us that the lowest-cost supplier is not always the best choice. When selecting suppliers, reliability, sustainability, and proximity are just as important as price. When suppliers and manufacturers share data, co-develop solutions, and collaborate on logistics, both will create new sources of cost savings and added-value opportunities.

The next layer of critical capability is the innovation/design-to-cost capability. My favorite saying is "design-to-cost, design-to-value, design-to-cash". When you introduce cost consciousness early in the design process, your product becomes more marketable without sacrificing value. I have seen product teams create new solutions using modular architecture, new materials, and digital products that deliver more value at lower cost by taking a creative approach to cost reduction.

Innovation isn't merely a 'nice to have' -- it's the most sustainable way of reducing costs. By using cost pressure as a driver for creativity, teams can turn constraints into innovation.

Financial Precision and ESG (Environmental, Social, and Governance) are also key to these capabilities. Financial precision is about holding ourselves accountable by using tools such as Earned Value Management (EVM), Return on Capital Employed (RoCE), and Life Cycle Costing (LCC) to turn cost tracking from a passive activity into an active discipline. Every rupee you spend should return something measurable or have a purpose. In today's world, financial precision must also include ESG. Sustainable cost management balances financial returns and environmental/social impact to ensure that companies protect their margins while safeguarding their long-term viability.

Near the top of the framework is ongoing benchmarking and learning. Competitiveness is not permanent, which is why organizations must continually measure themselves against peers and disruptors. I often recommend creating a "learning cost graph," a visual record of cost movements, savings, and reinvestments over time. Such learning loops prevent complacency and keep the organization alert, curious, and adaptive.

At the top of the pyramid lies strategic alignment, the culmination of all previous layers. Here, every decision, every product, every service aligns with a larger purpose. In my own leadership journey, this alignment has always come down to three words: Growth, Profitability, and Cash. When cost decisions support all three, organizations operate with clarity. When they don't, drift begins.

When the function of cost, value, and purpose align around these three pillars, then decision-making clarity emerges.

Every rupee saved enhances competitive advantage, and every rupee invested supports customer value rate. This is how cost becomes a competitive advantage rather than a barrier.

Connecting Cost to Customer Value

If there is one principle I have consistently adhered to throughout my career, it is this: **every cost decision must ultimately be tied to customer value.** The moment cost becomes detached from value; it ceases to be an investment and becomes an inefficiency.

I have seen leaders proudly cut costs, only to discover later that they were cutting muscle, not fat. The reality is that cost is neither inherently good nor bad; it depends on the reason for incurring it. When cost is aligned with customer value, it becomes an investment; when it comes from fear or short-term thinking, it is wasted.

The strategic question I believe every leader should ask before approving any cost is: "Will this increase/protect what the customer perceives as value?" If the answer isn't clear, the likely truth is it's a poor decision. The way to compete on cost is not to reduce costs, but to generate the maximum ROI per rupee spent.

To tie cost to value, I find it helpful to perform what I call value mapping by examining cost from three related, distinct viewpoints:

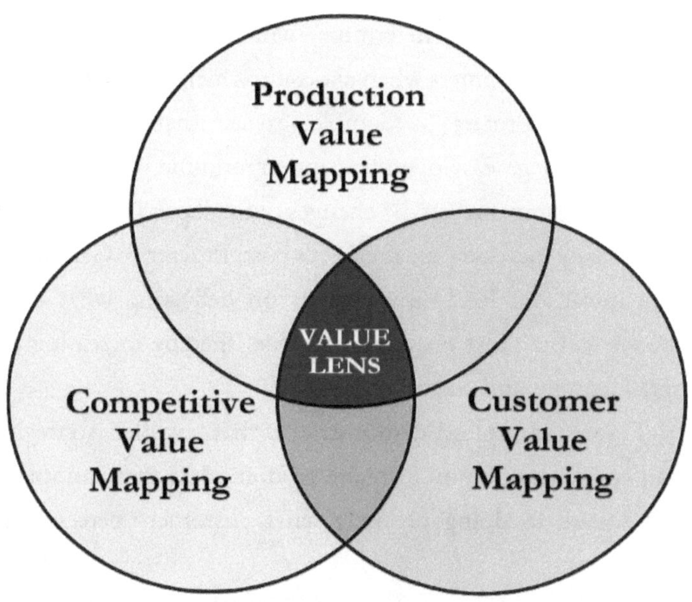

The Value Mapping Triad

Where these three maps converge, we will find the "value lens" through which we should evaluate any cost decisions. This is not a finance tool; this is a leadership perspective.

Worldwide, the best organizations have achieved this linkage. For example, Toyota has an excellent understanding of the relationship between cost reduction and value creation; it views its philosophy of "Genchi Genbutsu" as the core of its cost-reduction process. Toyota believes that every decision about costs should be made in direct observation, testing, or understanding of how that cost impacts the customer's experience. The company does not reduce costs solely to cut costs; instead, Toyota reduces waste that customers would never pay for.

Similarly, Procter & Gamble has developed its own value-mapping process to determine which product attributes are important to consumers when choosing which products to purchase. For example, Procter & Gamble learned that specific packaging innovations (e.g., easy-open lids and ergonomic grips) created more value for consumers than did changes to small parts of its formula that substantially increased the product's cost. Procter & Gamble focused its financial and R&D investments on delivering what customers perceive as the most outstanding value, thereby increasing both its overall margins and customer loyalty.

These examples demonstrate that while strategic cost competitiveness does not equate to doing less than competitors, it does equate to doing precisely what customers perceive as most valuable.

In India, there are unique situations where I have witnessed this. An example is the Tata Ace Tiny Truck. This tiny workhorse truck has come to symbolize low price with solid, rugged reliability, and during the product development stages of the Tata Ace, team members continually challenged their preconceived notions of what small-business vehicle owners needed in this vehicle. When studying small-scale vehicle owners, an overwhelming preference is found for load capacity, durability, and the ease of repair versus speed and/or interior comforts. Cost decisions/metrics were based on that perspective. What could small-scale entrepreneurs benefit from? The result of this approach was a vehicle with unprecedented value for every rupee spent on operating a small business, and it fundamentally transformed the light commercial vehicle market.

The most significant thing from the story is how to define customer value precisely, which leads to waste in many forms, including financial, emotional, effort, and opportunity costs.

When leaders link every cost to perceived value, they no longer have to manage budgets; instead, they manage meaning. Therefore, this produces increased loyalty and sustainable margins, and results in a business that customers and employees instinctively trust.

Culture

After working in the industry for many years, I've found that well-thought-out cost strategies are unsustainable in a company culture that doesn't support them. While systems and tools do help align processes, only culture can align people. When it comes to cost competitiveness, culture isn't a secondary factor—it is your competitive advantage.

Culture will determine whether a company's employees view cost as an impediment to their success or a creative opportunity. I have seen two extremes in the industry: one company that feared cost conversations because of the blame, budget cuts, and restrictions that would follow, while another company encouraged employees to find new ways to improve efficiency by sharing their cost-reduction ideas. What made the difference between these two companies? The companies had very different cultures.

A fear culture looks at cost management as a punitive measure, as something that is mandated in times of hardship, a burden to be borne in exchange for keeping one's job. In addition to this fear, people will retreat, hide their knowledge, refuse to take responsibility, and act with caution rather than creativity. The result does not create savings; it creates silence. As decisions are delayed and issues are contended with, managers must now only manage the shadows of what is actually occurring.

On the other hand, the cost culture promotes responsibility rather than restriction. It encourages employees to identify waste because improved efficiency is seen as a mark of professional pride rather than a mandate from management. For many years, I have advised teams to "repose confidence, not create scarcity thinking." When employees are working from a state of confidence, they will openly share information, suggest ways to improve processes and practices, and consider a culture that focuses on cost discipline as a source of collective strength. This change of perspective transforms cost optimization from a fear-based activity to a company-wide habit.

The core principle of this culture is what I call the "Value Per Rupee" mentality. Long-term competitive advantage is not achieved by reducing spending, but by increasing it more effectively. While saving is essential, creating value is more important. I have seen firsthand how accurately this mentality is represented on the shop floor. In many factories, employees would mark on a whiteboard the units of output they lost for the day and convert them into rupees. This was not required of them; it became their new definition of success. When people voluntarily pay for items, it is a visible sign of a cultural shift from compliance to ownership.

"Modeling" is a key component of this transition, as it supports the development of individual workplace culture. Workplace culture does not start with slogans and posters; it starts with the actions and behavior of the organization's leaders when their audience isn't watching, or when the organization doesn't intend to convey any message. Instead of focusing on opulence and excess, leadership should center on demonstrating utility in everything they invest in and on providing a rationale for their investments. The transparency and visibility of cost-conscious decisions should be shared with the team, enabling them to understand the decision's rationale. During one of the factories visits I made, I observed leadership using basic posters that depicted the linkage between technical parameters and bottom-line impact. The results of this simple technique were spectacular; I saw operators, many of whom had never identified with "strategy," recognize that their daily activities contributed value to the organization.

When workers view their jobs as more than just an obligation, culture becomes a competitive advantage. That's also when the cost of doing business shifts from "a number" to a relationship. Cost then becomes part of the language of purpose, pride, and common ambition.

In the early stages of my steel industry career, I was confronted with a lesson that profoundly affected my understanding of cost management, fundamentally changing my approach. A large volume of high-silica limestone had been stacked for eventual disposal, as it was conventionally believed to be of no value in conventional production. The assumption was simple — if the material did not meet the specifications for accepted use, it had to be thrown away.

However, rather than accepting this assumption, I sought to dive deep. Upon analysis, it was determined that this high-silica limestone could be used in the blast furnace by partially replacing quartzite, as it can contribute to the slag in place of quartzite with some yield reduction, while preserving metallurgical quality when charged in a controlled manner. When viewed as a whole, the outcome was not what would normally be expected; instead, it was compelling: overall waste was significantly reduced, and material utilization improved, leading to a reduction in overall costs.

This change in thinking took cultural courage — to have the guts to question long-held beliefs, to replace convenience with clarity, and to prefer the long-term efficiency of the entire system over short-term comfort and convenience. I learned that precision is not just an analytical skill but also a cultural attribute.

A cost framework succeeds when culture carries it forward. It's culture that sustains precision, enforces discipline, and inspires belief. When people start seeing cost competitiveness not as compliance, but as a contribution, it becomes the ultimate differentiator, a weapon that no competitor can easily copy.

Frameworks in Action

A framework, no matter how elegant, has no power until it's lived. Implementation is where clarity meets discipline. Over the years, I've learned that rolling out a strategic cost framework isn't about enforcing new rules; it's about aligning people, processes, and priorities so that everyone moves in sync. I often describe implementation as **a wheel of alignment**. At the center of the wheel are leadership clarity and intent. Around it are four reinforcing spokes: processes, metrics, communication, and culture. When all four turn together, the organization gains momentum; when one breaks, progress wobbles.

Cascading from Top to Bottom

Implementation starts with leadership, but it cannot end there. I've seen frameworks fail because they were kept at the top, discussed in boardrooms, but never translated for the frontline.

The intention is to translate the leadership vision into reality for employees at all levels. To enable this vision, leaders must be transparent about the costs involved in becoming competitive. Only then can they successfully develop the mechanisms needed to achieve competitiveness. It is common for leaders to articulate their companies' visions with clarity. Therefore, I maintain that the vision's structure must be evident throughout the entire organization — not just as a document, but as the way of conducting business. Employees in every department should be aware of how their work contributes to the organization's growth, profitability, and cash flow. When leaders have a clear vision, it is the responsibility of middle management to determine how to implement it, and ultimately the responsibility of front-line employees to execute it.

Implementation is tuning an engine. If you view each department as an engine cylinder, then all the cylinders must fire together to enhance overall performance. This is one reason that I advocate gradual implementation. Establish the framework as a pilot in a single unit, supporting this unit by advancing through a methodical approach based on your experience. Eventually, you would make the framework a permanent part of your business by creating structures that support its implementation, such as scorecards, feedback loops, and recognition systems. Establishing a rhythm will help develop buy-in so that employees see the framework not as a passing trend, but as an effective system for achieving results. As long as departments use different standards to assess success, the accuracy of performance metrics will be compromised; therefore, a company needs to establish a single form of truth, including a standard dashboard with clear indicators for all company- and departmental-level performance metrics. One example of this can be found in one of my experiences, where the finance department reported a savings level. In contrast, operations reported the same expense line item as a negative performance. After we developed a shared dashboard that displayed the same performance metrics for both departments, the conversation shifted from defending numbers to collaborating on resolving issues. This is the true power of shared visibility.

A prime example of this concept on a worldwide scale is IKEA. Their network not only includes internal systems but also includes their entire network, including designers, suppliers, logistics, and consumers. Every one of these points or interactions was mapped against both cost and value. Therefore, the price one sees listed on IKEA products is not the result of a random price discount; it is the result of intentional, exacting processes in design, sourcing, packaging, and logistics. The way IKEA leverages its organizational structure enables rather than limits creativity. IKEA uses the same structure to redefine what constraints are, rewriting the concept of constraints as design challenges, and fostering both innovative and competitive behavior simultaneously.

Measuring and Sustaining the Framework

After establishing a cost–value framework, the real work comes in sustaining it. I have witnessed many organizations develop great dashboards, conduct reviews, etc., but then once the excitement wears off, they lose momentum and discontinue their value measurement efforts. To maintain accuracy, you need particular measurement criteria.

Metrics That Matter

I typically categorize Key Result Indicators (KRIs) and Key Performance Indicators (KPIs). KRIs tell us what happened as far as profitability, reducing costs, improving customer satisfaction; KPI's tell us why it happened, i.e., efficiency in processes, defect rate, vendor reliability, etc. Leaders can connect results to specific actions, behaviors, and other factors by analyzing comprehensive metrics.

When an organization's supply chain becomes more efficient (fewer deliveries) but complaints increase, the metrics will show that efficiency was achieved at the expense of value. Therefore, accurate measurement across the entire operation is critical; the only part of the operation you will be able to connect back to its impact will be those measured against activity.

A robust measurement system should use three sets of dimensions:

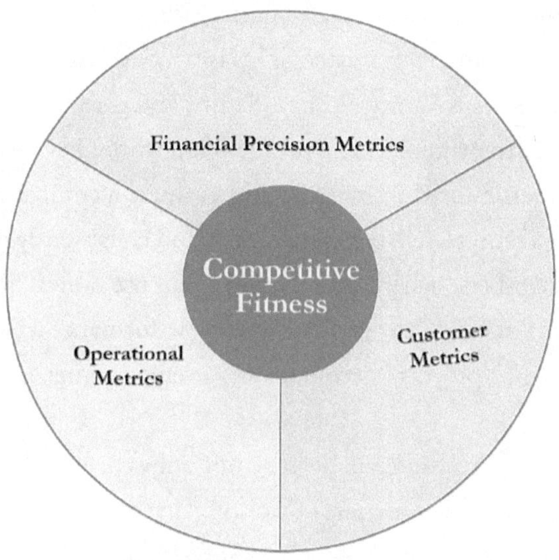

360⁰ Performance

The DuPont Logic and the Value Creation Trilogy

One of the fundamental ideas in management is the DuPont Model. The three drivers of profitability according to this model are margin, asset efficiency, and leverage. This simple model reminds us that achieving growth is not merely about reducing expenses; it is about leveraging our assets to produce the greatest return possible with the least capital.

When trying to help teams understand how to use these components, I use a framework that I refer to as the Value Creation Trilogy:

- Growth to create expanded opportunities.
- Profitability to ensure delivery efficiency; and
- Cash provides an element of stability and flexibility for an organization.

If a particular decision does not improve at least one of these components or, worse, actually harms any of them. It should be turned around and re-evaluated. This is why I constantly remind my teams that "Sales is Vanity, Profit is Sanity, and Cash is Reality"; these phrases help to maintain focus on the framework I have established.

The metrics used to measure and evaluate a company's progress need to be accurate, reliable, transparent, and consistently reviewed by all team members. When team members can use honest, reliable, and transparent metrics to evaluate their performance regularly, the improvement process becomes an everyday mentality for all employees.

This way, Precision will become not only a project, but a culture.

When I look back at years of working on cost transformation, one truth stands out clearly: structure creates strength.

Competitiveness doesn't emerge from isolated cost-cutting efforts; it comes from a disciplined framework that integrates cost, value, and culture into a unified system of intent.

Simplifying the complicated decision-making process within an organization is the first step. Connecting and identifying to what each rupee is spent on creates an outcome, what it protects, and what inefficiencies it eliminates, clarifying the view throughout an organization as it pertains to cost management. Cost management is no longer limited to the finance function; rather, it is an enterprise-wide, team-driven endeavor within an aligned organization. Cost competitiveness is achieved through this alignment and a shared vision across the organization at all levels (leadership, operations, sourcing, and design). These consistent views of decision-making allow organizations to make faster, sharper trade-offs and to convert organizational structure to intelligence. Even though frameworks allow organizations to develop the capabilities necessary to integrate cost management, a framework does not sustain itself; a company's culture enables it. Cultural values drive behavior. Cultural values make cost awareness an ingrained behavior, enabling teams to achieve value-creating events as quickly as they achieve sales wins. Ultimately, the value created by a framework is not limited to how much cost it has removed. Still, to the extent it enables the organization to create maximum value with each rupee, allows for growth without waste, fosters innovation without excess, and operates with purpose and precision.

Cost competitiveness today is not about trimming the present; it is about funding the future. When an organization learns to remove waste without sacrificing capability, cost becomes a constraint rather than an advantage. For ESG/ sustainability, True cost competitiveness is sustainable-it preserves resources, protects future value, and strengthens trust.

For me, that's the essence of strategic cost competitiveness: structure, alignment, and culture working in harmony. When these three converge, organizations don't just survive competition; they define it.

Before moving on, you should pause and draw your current cost decision-making process not on a laptop or in a PowerPoint slide, but on a piece of paper or a whiteboard. Influential people do not need a

PowerPoint presentation to establish their viewpoint. Sketch it as it exists today.

When making cost decisions, who is the first to call, which departments are included, and when does the customer have a voice in the conversation? As you begin creating your map, you'll quickly notice an area where the value lens seems to disappear - this is one of your most significant opportunities. After you do this for each business unit/project using the Cost-Value Strategic Framework, you should apply the framework to each business unit or project. You should identify:

- Where transparency is lacking
- Where operational discipline should be improved
- How design/sourcing could better align with the customer's priority
- Where culture, communication, or measurement is out of alignment

The purpose of this exercise is to eliminate guesswork and create structure; however, the framework must be lived to be effective. The first step in this process is to visualize your organization's current perspective of cost/value.

I always say, "When you put structure around cost thinking, what becomes visible are the good, bad, and invisible patterns." It is at this point where real advancement occurs. Strategic cost competitiveness enables you to view your business as a single, connected system rather than just a collection of line-item expenses.

When you develop a framework for cost, it enables every rupee, decision, and improvement you make to fit into a much larger business narrative - a narrative in which cost becomes the language of Value.

However, while gaining clarity from structure is immensely helpful for establishing stability, it ultimately does not serve the purpose of maintaining relevancy in the competitive landscape we operate in today. The markets will constantly shift. Technological advancements will create new opportunities and force you to change your business models to meet new customer demands; therefore, having a framework in place will help you respond to those changes. But the real question is: what is your source of innovation?

The answer is Innovation. The next significant milestone for your business is not only to operate your existing model effectively but also to innovate and reimagine it. The most significant breakthroughs I have had the opportunity to witness occurred when teams used the pressure of costs to create new ways of thinking about how they do business, ultimately developing an innovative growth mindset.

Chapter 4
The Innovation Multiplier

From my experience, I understand how companies behave (both differently and similarly) during a downturn. Generally speaking, many companies take on a 'freeze' approach; after cutting back on all resources, they wait until the economy improves and they can recover financially. This typically means that the majority of discussions in these meetings revolve around what cannot be done rather than what could be achieved. Employees begin defending their jobs and paychecks today, rather than designing and developing products and services for tomorrow.

However, I have also been fortunate enough to work with some companies/people who take the opposite approach when their resources decrease. When resources become scarce, these companies create new things and find new ways to realize what was once only seen as possibilities, given the abundance of resources. For these companies, limited resources do not act as a hindrance; instead, they are a positive experience that creates new opportunities and sparks creativity.

I have had many experiences working with innovative companies that created significant change, but constraints drove that innovation. The majority of these innovations came from limitations such as limited funding to support research and development (R&D), limited time to develop the product or service, and limited certainty on the result of the R&D. I have seen engineers turn a material shortage into a revolutionary product; I have seen supply chain managers create completely new delivery routes following the traditional routes becoming too expensive to support.

I have seen many startups grow into national companies operating on budgets that would not allow for a single corporate event.

Reflecting on some of the most formative times in my life, I have been struck by one common thread: limitations stimulate imagination; stress stimulates opportunity.

Though this may seem counterintuitive, there is something intuitive about how lack forces the brain to focus. When there are few available options left, other paths become visible (though sometimes completely unrelated to the original). Learning how to take advantage of limited opportunities can bring clarity, creative thinking, and more courageous choices.

Throughout history, countless innovative solutions have been developed out of necessity during challenging times, rather than when conditions were "ideal." As I have experienced numerous examples of this same phenomenon in the Indian Industry, there were several occasions when constraints gave rise to creative new ways of working; when otherwise these new solutions would not have come about due to the ineffectiveness of too many resources (including money). In such scenarios, and when viewed as an opportunity and not as a threat, cost-reduction pressures serve as a multiplier for innovation within the organization, as they create:

1. New process designs.
2. A fresh perspective on past assumptions.
3. Maximization of existing capabilities; and
4. A focus on the actual needs of customers (as opposed to a projected need).

The innovation multiplier is the capacity to turn resource pressures into advantages for creativity.

When organizations learn to view constraints as opportunities rather than limitations, innovation stops being episodic and becomes systematic.

One of the most common myths in organizations is that innovation requires a great deal of money.

We equate it with cutting-edge laboratories, evolving research and development centers, large budgets, and lengthy development cycles. Unfortunately, this mindset creates stagnation for many companies rather than a competitive advantage.

The fact is that innovation thrives under circumstances of limited resources. When available resources limit you, it forces you to eliminate anything unnecessary, rethink every assumption, and focus on the root of the issue. That clarity can be very effective in focusing on the core of the problem and in prompting teams to generate ideas differently, using better ideas rather than larger budgets as the basis for decision-making.

Innovation isn't about futuristic prototypes or moonshot projects. It's about solving meaningful problems in smarter, simpler, and more scalable ways. It is the discipline of creating value where others only see limitations.

The central concept is that the Innovation Multiplier equals the sum of cost pressure, creativity, and value alignment. Businesses can expand despite budget cuts thanks to this multiplier. It transforms limitations into chances for reimagining. It turns operational difficulties into unique selling points.

Innovation becomes a method of thinking ingrained in everyday choices, front-line problem-solving, leadership intent, and cultural habits rather than an event or a department. Having a proper mindset, structures, and practices in place will allow constraints to create the environment for the most significant breakthrough innovations.

Companies that view budget cuts as an opportunity to rethink, redesign, and reimagine their next generation do not fear these inevitable challenges.

Debunking the Myth of "Innovation is Expensive"

I have observed for many years that when the topic of innovation is mentioned, there is an immediate shift in attention to the Chief Financial Officer, and the first person to respond is often the one who says, "budget limitations." Someone else usually adds, "Let's save this discussion until next quarter." The primary understanding is that substantial financial investments must fund innovation, access cutting-edge technology, or have a dedicated R&D division; otherwise, no company with limited resources can truly be "innovative."

I've always found this assumption misleading. Innovation doesn't necessarily need money. Innovation needs intent.

Groundbreaking ideas I've seen come from people who weren't working with bigger budgets but had better clarity. They saw what needed fixing and had an insatiable desire to find alternative ways to fix it.

The misconception that innovation costs a lot of money stems from confusing two very different processes: R&D-focused innovation and the everyday innovations carried out by companies or individuals. R&D-focused innovation is expensive, and most people know that. Everyday innovation (which also tends to have the most significant impact) requires curiosity, the ability to look at things and see what needs to be changed, and an openness to trying new things (experimentation). I frequently recall the Apollo 13 mission, when NASA engineers used duct tape and spare parts to create an improvised carbon dioxide filter.

They lacked equipment, time, and money. They had a clear issue and a constraint. That limitation stimulated creativity.

Nearer to home, have a look at the numerous examples of economical engineering in the Indian industry.

I've witnessed engineers redo process stages to remove waste, alter materials to save costs while increasing strength, or rethink assemblies to employ fewer parts. None of these necessitated large expenditures. They demanded a different way of thinking.

Take the Tata Nano, one of the most ambitious frugal engineering efforts the world has witnessed; the engineering effort itself proved a vital point: innovation doesn't always mean adding more. Sometimes, it means stripping away everything that doesn't matter.

True innovation asks a simple question: "What is the simplest, smartest way to solve this problem?"

It may involve a new idea, a novel combination of existing ideas, or a more effective way of applying what we already know. Most importantly, it doesn't wait for perfect conditions. If anything, it appears when conditions are far from perfect.

> I remind leaders of this constantly: If your innovation strategy begins with money, it will also end with money. If it begins with insight, it will end with impact, because innovation is not expensive. Innovation is simply the discipline of solving problems boldly and resourcefully, even when budgets are tight.
> But *Inefficiency* is expensive. *Inaction* is expensive. *Fear* is expensive.

The Power of Constraints

Individuals with more clarity and the motivation to find new and better ways to resolve issues, not necessarily individuals with more financial resources, created many of the most innovative solutions

I have seen in various locations, including manufacturing, logistics, and quality control.

Equating two different definitions of innovation—industry-specific research and development-led discoveries, which can need substantial financial commitment, and general innovation, where most impact is achieved—leads to the false assumption that innovation will be costly. The former cannot survive without financial support. A person's curiosity, capacity to notice their surroundings, and willingness to take certain risks through experimentation all significantly contribute to the latter.

The constraints we face force us to determine what is critical within the problem or issue before moving ahead to design. For example, when a manufacturer thinks of redesigning a product that has become too expensive for the market, the typical response is to reduce the number of features. Rather than pursuing this line of thought, the design team reframed the constraint: "What if we could achieve the same value with fewer pieces?"

The end product of the redesign had significantly fewer parts than before, was easier to assemble, and performed better in the field. Rather than limiting possible solutions due to constraints, the redesign actually expanded the design possibilities. Therefore, I often explain, "Without constraints, there is no canvas, only canvas for creativity."

Constraints also force organizations to be precise. When you don't have the luxury of excess, your decisions become sharper. You prioritize outcomes, not activities. You measure what actually matters. And you value ideas from anywhere in the organization, not just from "innovation teams."

> I often run a simple exercise with leaders: "If your budget were cut by 50%, how would you redesign your process? What would you stop doing? What would you simplify?"

The answers are often far more innovative than what teams propose when budgets are healthy. In fact, several creative business models have emerged in response to limitations, such as Toyota's lean manufacturing system during the post-war shortage period and Southwest Airlines' model under severe cost pressure. Due to their lack of resources to set up traditional distribution channels, Indian companies were able to provide same-day local delivery through community networks. Limitations are uncomfortable. However, they are truthful. They make it precise what really counts. They reveal inefficiencies. They are creative. Additionally, they transform regular teams into creative teams because innovation is unavoidable. The most excellent resource an organization can have is not abundance. It is clarity under constraint.

Lean Innovation Practices

When people think of innovation, they assume it will be a large, polished solution.

However, I have found that the best ideas do not begin with this level of polish; they start as rough prototypes, tests, and experiments. Lean Innovation is about learning, building, and iterating fast.

Lean innovation is not about perfection; it's about being productive with intention on your path to success.

MVPs (Minimum Viable Product), prototypes, and rapid learning encourage testing of ideas as early as possible, rather than waiting for them to be perfect, and uncover real information through low-cost tests and prototypes.

Lean Innovation also acknowledges that you will not know what works until you test it. The 'Good-to-Have' vs. the 'Must-Have' filter provides you with a means to prioritize features and demonstrate that there are many 'appreciable' features in your product that you cannot afford to produce when budgets shrink.

Innovation occurs outside the confines of the R&D department. It happens every single day through the redesign of jigs, the renaming of suppliers, and the changing of supply chains, demonstrating that big ideas drive progress, not big budgets.

Lean innovation becomes powerful when it becomes everyday behavior, not an annual event.

Lean innovation is not just about saving money; it is about concentrating on what is necessary. It is also not about having a limited supply of resources. Instead, it focuses on innovative ordering, quick cycles, and continual education. Once you've started thinking this way about your company's innovation processes, it will stop being an exception, and it will become the norm for your organization.

Linking Innovation to Cost Competitiveness

One of the most common errors I observe is treating innovation and cost competitiveness as distinct concepts, with innovation seen favorably and cost competitiveness seen unfavorably.

In reality, the most effective innovations are those that increase value while reducing expenses.

Innovation becomes a multiplier in this situation. Competitiveness increases when limitations spur innovation, and innovation increases value. The way this multiplier actually functions in an organization is explained in the framework that follows.

What It Looks Like	What It Really Means
Cost as an Expense	A lost opportunity, money saved without value created.
Cost as an Investment	Spending that increases value per rupee; innovation tied to competitive advantage.
Product Innovation	New features. New variants. New colors.
Process Innovation	Waste elimination, simplification, automation, and flow efficiency are the real sources of sustainable gains.
Cutting Costs in Isolation	Short-term relief, long-term fragility, customer value erosion.
Redesigning Value Delivery	Logistics partnerships, flow redesign, subscription models, smarter delivery at lower cost.
Resource Constraints	Supposed limitations.
Innovation Multiplier	Constraints → Creativity → Value Expansion → Market Competitiveness.

Innovation frequently starts with the discipline of cost clarity rather than costly labs or ground-breaking technologies. Teams' creativity becomes more impactful, focused, and grounded when they view costs as investments rather than expenses.

For example, process innovation has generally produced longer-lasting efficiency improvements than product features. Value may be unlocked without raising costs by rethinking delivery strategies from logistical networks to subscription services. When budget limitations become creative opportunities, that's when the true magic happens.

This is how the innovation multiplier works: cost pressure encourages more creative thinking, which increases value and boosts competitiveness.

The Mindset for Innovation Under Pressure

In every organization I've worked with, innovation doesn't start with money, tools, or technology. It starts with a leadership mindset. When leaders treat constraints as obstacles, the entire organization becomes defensive. But when leaders treat constraints as challenges to be solved, the organization becomes inventive. Constraints don't create innovation. Leaders do so through the mindset they model.

Because they don't view boundaries as dead ends, confident leaders flourish under duress. They see them as cues. Leaders in consumer goods, manufacturing, healthcare, and logistics have approached resource scarcity with a spirit of constructive curiosity: "What if we simplify this design?" or "Instead of investing more, can we partner differently?" or "Is it possible to provide the same value in fewer steps?"

One great example of innovative thinking under pressure is Narayana Healthcare, which managed to innovate while operating under intense cost constraints and refusing to compromise on the quality of care. Instead of simply using a cost-cutting strategy, Narayana has rethought how it delivers care by standardizing processes, creating efficient workflows, and leveraging scale to reduce the average cost of a procedure. The need for cost-effectiveness has led Narayana to create a Continuous Follow-Up System that supports a collaborative culture of intelligent redesign. This more significant achievement speaks to the truth that when two or more factors pose a challenge, challenge-related solutions generally drive progress towards institutional excellence, rather than retreating into the pressure zone.

To foster a culture of institutional excellence, you must create an environment that allows leaders to tolerate failure and to innovate through calculated risk-taking. The process of innovation under pressure is not about taking risks unthinkingly – it is about allowing leaders the freedom to experiment. For example, teams must feel they are not penalized for trying something new and failing during their initial attempts to create innovative solutions. As a result, when mistakes are punished in an organization, creativity will recede into silence. In contrast, in cultures where leadership promotes learning through doing, employees will be encouraged to innovate with confidence through collaboration, and psychological safety will be the unspoken force keeping ideas alive.

The people closest to a problem are typically the ones with the most remarkable ability to create effective solutions. Machine operators, supervisors, drivers, quality assurance analysts, and procurement coordinators face resource constraints every day. They identify inefficiencies in operational processes—often not visible in reports—and create solutions to make their jobs easier without ever asking the executive team for help. When organizations actively ask for and engage all employees, they develop a system that enables employees to collaborate on innovation rather than being limited to the traditional innovation process used in an elite studio. The ultimate goal is to create a culture where everyone has the opportunity to contribute and collaborate to create innovative products and services. I have personally experienced this in organizations that have evolved their standard suggestion programs into opportunities to transform the organization. One suggestion to move a workstation resulted in the organization saving thousands of hours of labor; another to redesign packaging saved millions in shipping costs. Neither of these revolutionary ideas came from the organization's senior leaders.

Instead, they came from employees on the ground who needed to be empowered to think outside the square.

However, while bottom-up innovations are valuable, they aren't enough on their own. If leaders are to embed their organization's innovations further, they should completely reframe what they celebrate. Most organizations celebrate large-scale launches, awards for large-scale innovation, and large-scale technological innovation(s) while missing the more minor yet impactful change(s) that can ultimately drive the most significant change(s) in an organization's culture. A significant shift occurs when leaders begin to celebrate the more minor "quiet victories." The small daily victories may include redesigning a fixture to eliminate seconds per cycle, reducing the time needed to complete a project, or making simple adjustments to improve safety. At some point, each small success creates momentum; the accumulated momentum builds the organization's belief in its ability to succeed. Over time, the accumulating momentum drives cultural change throughout the organization; thus, innovation becomes embedded in the organization's standard operating procedures.

Leadership mindset is the ignition point of the Innovation Multiplier. When leaders show courage, curiosity, and humility under constraint, the organization responds with creativity, discipline, and pride. That is how innovation grows roots.

Building a Culture of Cost-Aware Innovation

A single innovative idea can have a significant impact. But a culture of innovation can transform an entire organization.

For innovation to thrive, especially in a resource-constrained environment, it must be embedded into daily routines, behaviors, and shared beliefs.

*Culture is not what organizations **say**. Culture is what organizations **celebrate**.*

An Innovation Culture is never derived from complex systems; it emerges when simple, obvious behaviors encourage all employees who are willing to share ideas and participate in innovation efforts. A High-Performance Manufacturing Facility will include items like Idea Walls, Kaizen Boards, or Suggestion Corners.

Unlike decorations hung on the wall, they are used as living and working areas where employees submit their issues and solutions to the problems they face. In these facilities, employees are recording their ideas each month and tracking them for their own benefit; not because they feel that they are required to track them, but rather because they have a direct visual representation of how their idea has positively impacted something.

If employees' submissions and the content displayed on these websites become "visible" to all employees, innovation will become a "natural" element of every business. It is not money that drives employees to submit ideas. It is their desire for identity.

Employees want to be known as people who can contribute to their company's success. This is why companies often find that symbolic recognition (Town Hall meeting mentions, framed "Innovation Spotlight" Photos, or framed "Zero-Cost Hero" Plaques) is more meaningful to employees than financial rewards or bonuses.

These symbolic recognitions help turn innovation from a one-time event into an ongoing source of pride for everyone in the company when they have been awarded/won that recognition.

Knowledge is transferred and built upon to provide momentum to this pride.

The most successful organizations utilize each of their improvements as a micro-case study (one-page story), detailing the challenge, idea, experiment, and outcome.

These micro-case studies initially circulate internally among the organization's teams as progress reports. As the micro-case studies circulate among teams, they help create a collective memory of the organization's collective work. This collective memory, along with the catalogue of problems solved and opportunities achieved, forms the organization's engine for innovation.

Over time, the organization's culture develops. Innovation is no longer a scheduled event but has become a daily commitment by all employees. Supervisors will adjust workflows; technicians will modify fixtures; drivers will enhance delivery routes. All employees view restrictions and limitations as opportunities to foster greater innovation. Once all employees embrace this view, the organization's rhythm will continue to be driven by continual innovation.

Measuring Innovation Success

One of the most prominent mistakes organizations make is measuring innovation solely by significant outcomes, such as product launches, breakthrough technologies, and cost savings in the crores.

Those matters, of course, but if that's all you measure, you miss the real heartbeat of innovation.

Category	Metric	What It Measures	Examples / How to Use It
VALUE METRICS *"What impact did this idea create?"*	**Value per rupee improved**	How efficiently does value increase relative to cost?	Compare ₹ spent vs. impact created (e.g., improved uptime, reduced defects).

	Cost avoided or reduced.	Direct & indirect savings generated.	Lower rework costs, less scrap, and reduced warranty claims.
	Customer satisfaction improvements	How the idea improved customer experience.	Higher NPS (Net Promoter Score), fewer complaints, faster resolution times.
	Throughput or defect reduction	Operational performance gains.	Shorter cycle times, fewer quality errors, and higher output with the same resources.
EFFORT METRICS *"How fast and how collectively did we learn?"*	**Number of experiments run**	Volume of real-world tests conducted.	Track experiments per team/unit per month.
	Learning cycle-time	Speed of idea → prototype → feedback → revision.	Reduce cycle time from weeks to days.
	Idea velocity	The momentum of experimentation across the org.	Measures participation and energy behind innovation initiatives.
ADOPTION METRICS *"Did people actually use the innovation?"*	**Percentage of ideas scaled.**	How many pilots have been completed?	Rollout rate across plants, branches, or teams.
	Cross-functional adoption	Spread of the idea across departments.	E.g., sourcing adopts an idea originating in manufacturing.
	Internal NPS of the innovation program	Whether employees find the system meaningful and	Pulse survey asking: "How likely are you to recommend

		worth investing in.	participating in this?"
IDEA QUALITY METRICS *"Are we solving the right problems?"*	**Value-to-effort ratio**	Impact is achievable for the effort required.	High-value, low-effort ideas get priority.
	Problem relevance index	Whether the idea tackles a critical business issue.	Rank ideas on strategic relevance before approving.
	Repeatability score	Scalability across geographies or units.	Can the idea be replicated at 10 plants or only 1?
INTEGRITY CHECK: *"Is this true innovation or just activity?"*	**Improves quality?**	Reliability, safety, consistency.	Yes/No check.
	Improves scalability?	Ability to expand without loss of quality.	Yes/No check.
	Improves participation?	Whether the idea increases engagement.	Yes/No check.
	If any answer is 'no' → it's not innovation.	Ensures discipline and honesty in evaluation.	Eliminates "activity disguised as innovation."

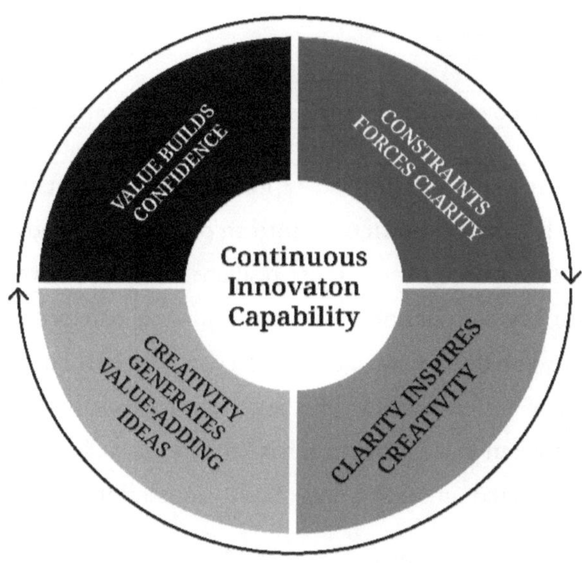

The Innovation Multiplier Model

When most people consider innovation, they likely envision significant improvements. Whereas the Innovation Multiplier does not involve large steps, it instead revolves around compounding. The flywheel effect demonstrated by the Innovation Multiplier shows that minor concepts can create extreme value when executed efficiently and effectively on a small scale, yielding significant returns and lower overall costs for consumers. The basic concept behind the Innovation Multiplier is the cost-pressure creativity chain reaction. Cost pressure on teams forces them to be more innovative, which, over time, creates greater value for their customers and therefore makes them much more competitive than their peers. As a result, when teams apply innovative approaches to solving real customer challenges, they provide additional value, enabling them to economically outperform their competitors because they incur no increase in the cost of their product offering.

The Cost–Value:

	Value Low	Value High
Cost Flat or Lower	Efficiency improvements	**Innovation Multiplier**
Cost Higher	Wasteful growth	Premium innovation zone

The Innovation Multiplier represents the thought process that consistently converts restrictions into an organization's advantage.

As I think back on the most resilient companies I've partnered with, one key foundational idea continues to emerge: to be truly innovative, you don't need more funds; you need to focus your efforts more clearly on innovation. The best ideas are usually identified and developed when an organization has limited funds, is competing in a highly saturated market, and faces constraints that limit its innovation.

The following are my top recommendations for leaders to remember going forward:

Innovation is not the privilege of those with large budgets. It's the right and responsibility of those with large ambitions.

Innovation doesn't begin with how much money is available; it starts with clarity, courage, and purpose.

A company that uses constraints as a catalyst to create innovative solutions will not only survive during difficult economic times but also thrive (lead) during them.

They will continue to find innovative methods of building, delivering, designing, and operating by turning frugality into functional excellence and by creating teams that take pride in the value of what they create through thoughtful simplicity.

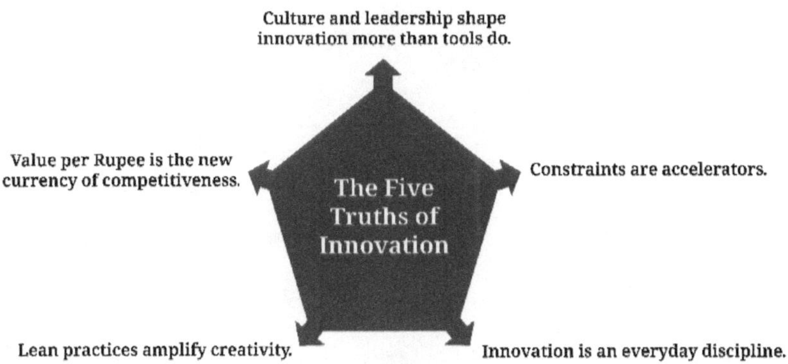

Finally, we must keep in mind that innovation is the only multiplier that compounds value faster than cost. A leadership role is not to drive innovation but to enable conditions where ideas multiply without permission. In fast-changing markets, innovation is not a differentiator- it is the entry ticket.

Chapter 5
Competing in The Indian Context

When I travel around India, I'm constantly reminded that there is no definitive version of this country; instead, it is an amalgamation of diverse markets, consumer behaviors, contradictions, and endless growth opportunities, all coexisting in unpredictable ways.

Take, for instance, a trip from a large metro area, where consumers want high levels of ease through digital interfaces and premium global experiences, to a smaller town an hour's drive away, where people discuss only price, product durability, consumer trust, and basic accessibility. You can shop at an upscale, high-end retail outlet in an upscale, urban mall and step outside to see someone purchasing a small item (₹2 worth) with cash because that's all they have available to them at any given moment. In one area, you might have an unbanked family living next door to someone who uses UPI as their primary form of payment.

I've seen numerous Global Brands enter India with all the confidence in the world, only to walk away confused and uncertain. What they believe to be premium positioning does not resonate. Their cost structures do not align. Their Value Propositions do not resonate with consumers. Moreover, they do not comprehend the complex emotional make-up of the Indian Consumer, who is:

- Highly price-conscious, strongly value-seeking
- Heavily Influenced by Trust & Community
- Hopeful & Aspiring

In addition, India has the largest population of Millennials and Gen Z, many of whom are Digital Natives and lack patience for disruptions in Legacy Systems. They also will not wait for those systems to catch up with their demands for instantaneous Banking, Online Shopping & Health Care, and their expectations have set a new definition of VALUE.

Another point of interest in the Indian Market is Informal Commerce, where millions of small family-owned businesses and hyper-local distribution systems function on Trust rather than Contracts. Additionally, the Policy and Governance Environment is continually changing, sometimes overnight, changing the Costs of Doing Business, Methods of Delivery, and Scaling Strategies.

In short, India demands cost-awareness, value sensitivity, digital adaptability, and emotional intelligence all at once. This chapter is about understanding that complexity. But more importantly, it's about learning how to win in it by blending frugality, creativity, and contextual innovation.

India as a Cost–Value Laboratory

While working across industries in India, I learned one thing for sure: India is the world's most significant testing ground for cost-to-value strategies. No other market puts the need to balance frugality, speed, innovation, and trust at such a high level. Some Western strategies assume stable income and infrastructure, and behaviors. India does not have this. India provides a much greater benefit than these assumptions suggest - it is a laboratory for learning how to build solutions in environments of uncertainty.

Indian Companies do not survive because they spend; Indian Companies survive because they think. They innovate under constraints, while creating value without excess.

They treat digital as an enabler and not an add-on. They collaborate informally, are flexible and adapt quickly, and build business models that both replicate and create significant depth at scale. When Companies are successful in India, they understand three things:

- Indian Consumers will only pay based on Value; what they can experience, trust, and justify.
- Frugality is a winning combination of competitive advantage and precision.
- Digital Tools make it possible to reach a much larger market at lower costs.

Understanding India's Cost–Value Landscape

India's market behaves in a manner unlike any other, and if you misunderstand this behavior, your strategy collapses before it even begins. To compete here, you must understand the underlying cost–value psychology that shapes every purchase decision from a sachet of shampoo to a mobile phone to a tractor.

India's Dual Market Reality

India is, by design, a "dual India." On the one hand, you have aspirational consumers in metropolitan areas who are willing to pay for convenience, speed, and lifestyle experiences. On the other hand, you have rural and semi-urban consumers, nearly 65% of the country's population, who evaluate every rupee based on durability, reliability, and trust.

These two markets coexist, overlap, and influence each other. A product that fails in rural India finds limited long-term scale in urban India. And a product that works in urban India must earn trust before it earns adoption elsewhere.

> **Urban India:** Aspirational • Convenience-seeking • Digital-first
> **Bharat:** Value-driven • Reliability-focused • Trust-led

Price Sensitive but Not Price Blind

One myth about India is that consumers are "cheap." That's not true. Indian consumers are value-literate. They do the mental math. They understand the total cost of ownership (TCO). They care about:

- Repairability
- Resale value
- Durability
- Serviceability
- And above all, trust.

A cheaper product without trust won't win. A costly product without perceived value won't survive. I often use the example of how Indian households trust certain brands, such as Tata Salt or Tata Besan, not only because they believe in the Tata Trust but also because Trust is a form of value here.

> *Price Sensitive ≠ Price Blind*
> India used **Total Cost of Ownership** long before the term existed.

Affordable, Reliable, Aspirational, Accessible

Over the years, I've come to see that India's value equation revolves around four anchors:

A	**Affordability** must fit the wallet.
R	**Reliability** must work consistently.
A	**Aspirational appeal** must make people feel proud.
A	**Accessibility** must be easy to buy, repair, and use.

Any product or service that nails these four wins disproportionately.

Why Competing on Cost Alone Fails

Many companies believe that representing India at a low price will attract customers and foster loyalty. This is a false assumption, because India rewards companies for providing both volume and quality, not just volume at low cost.

A company offering a low-cost product will fail if it compromises on quality, provides unreliable service, lacks a trusted brand, or fails to create an emotional connection with customers. There are two fatal mistakes companies serving the Indian Market Make.

Low-cost product + Unreliable service = failure	Premium-priced product + Unclear emotional value = failure

India's Competitive Edge

Frugal innovation and technology are the two characteristics of India's competitive advantage as an emerging economy. While in most countries' frugality is often equated with giving up something to be innovative, in India, frugality is a business strategy that incorporates a mix of engineering discipline, business acumen, and cultural intuition that allows organizations to provide services to many people with the least amount of resources - and at the same time, make progress in meaningful innovation.

Two of the main characteristics of India's position within the global economy are the combination of both instinctive and strategic frugality. From the outside, these two characteristics can seem simple; however, within India, both are incredibly sophisticated, highly precise, and ingeniously implemented.

Instinctive Frugality	Strategic Frugality
Survival-fueled grassroots creativity versus theoretical application of an idea. I've witnessed elegant examples of this in many different ways: • Tier 2 machining and manufacturing shops re-purposing tooling well beyond their expected cycles • Unorthodox supply chain creativity in creating add-on tooling • Locally operated businesses/system operators creating their own solutions to problems using hours (usually only minutes), not days of lead time These examples demonstrate that sophisticated solutions emerge from safety, driven by need.	Deliberate and engineered frugality represent the opposite end of the continuum from the day-to-day operational frugality we typically see in companies. Examples would include the following: • World-class surgeries are performed at Aravind Eye Care, priced significantly lower than comparable surgeries around the world. • The engineering team's mission is to minimize the component count of Tata Vehicles while maximizing functionality through scientific precision. • Tata Electric Bus, design approach that minimizes lifecycle costs; • Reliance Jio's revolutionary collapse of data prices changed the definition of digital access affordability in India. These examples represent the engineering of value, not cheapness; they blend design disciplines with empathy for customers.

India's Habit of Leapfrogging

One of India's greatest strengths is the ability to jump stages of development. We didn't go from landlines to better landlines; we skipped ahead to mobile phones. We didn't wait for credit card adoption to mature; we jumped directly to UPI.

I still remember discussing digital adoption with a farmer who said, "I don't understand banking forms, but I can send money on UPI in five seconds." That's India's superpower technology adoption, free from legacy baggage.

The Indian customer doesn't begin on a desktop. They begin and end on mobile. Even I, during vacations, no longer carry my laptop. Everything from ticketing to ordering groceries to checking factory dashboards can be done on a smartphone. And if this is the case for me, imagine the velocity of adoption in households that skipped the desktop era altogether.

Digital rails like UPI, FASTag, DigiLocker, and Aadhaar-enabled services aren't conveniences. They are cost reducers. They remove friction, eliminate intermediaries, collapse paperwork, and accelerate service delivery.

Vernacular Digital India

Vernacular content is another trend that is redefining India. From:

- ShareChat Building a Multi-Lingual Social Ecosystem
- DailyHunt Delivering Regional News to Millions
- Regional OTT Platforms Emerging
- AI-Based Translation Tools Enabling Cross-Language Commerce

Serving people in their language is a necessity, providing a link between access & adoption.

India's competitive strength is not just low cost. It is cost intelligence supported by a digital scale. This is why frugality plus digital together become a force multiplier, the combination that allows Indian businesses to compete in ways global companies often don't anticipate.

The Informal Sector and the Importance of Scale

To truly understand India, one must first understand the informal sector, which serves as more than just an additional component of the overall economy. Currently, the informal sector accounts for approximately 40% of India's GDP and employs approximately 75% of the labor force. Informal businesses are primarily based on developing & maintaining close relationships through interpersonal interactions between their employees and clients, and therefore rely heavily on the following principles: trust, local knowledge, community support, and a unique ability to respond immediately & successfully to changes in their environment.

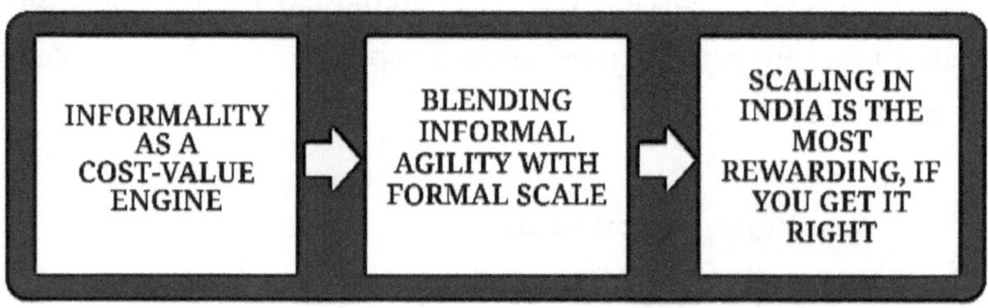

Although many view informalities as a disadvantage, these attributes provide India with a competitive advantage. The flexibility and adaptability afforded by informality, combined with the formal infrastructure provided by digital platforms, such as telecommunications and internet access, produce an environment in which informal business practices can flourish.

Policy, Infrastructure, and Governance

The government establishes India's policy framework through its legislative process. The Indian government creates policies to facilitate the establishment of business opportunities.

However, as is frequently the case in densely populated regions of the world, policy is sometimes created with contradictory intent.

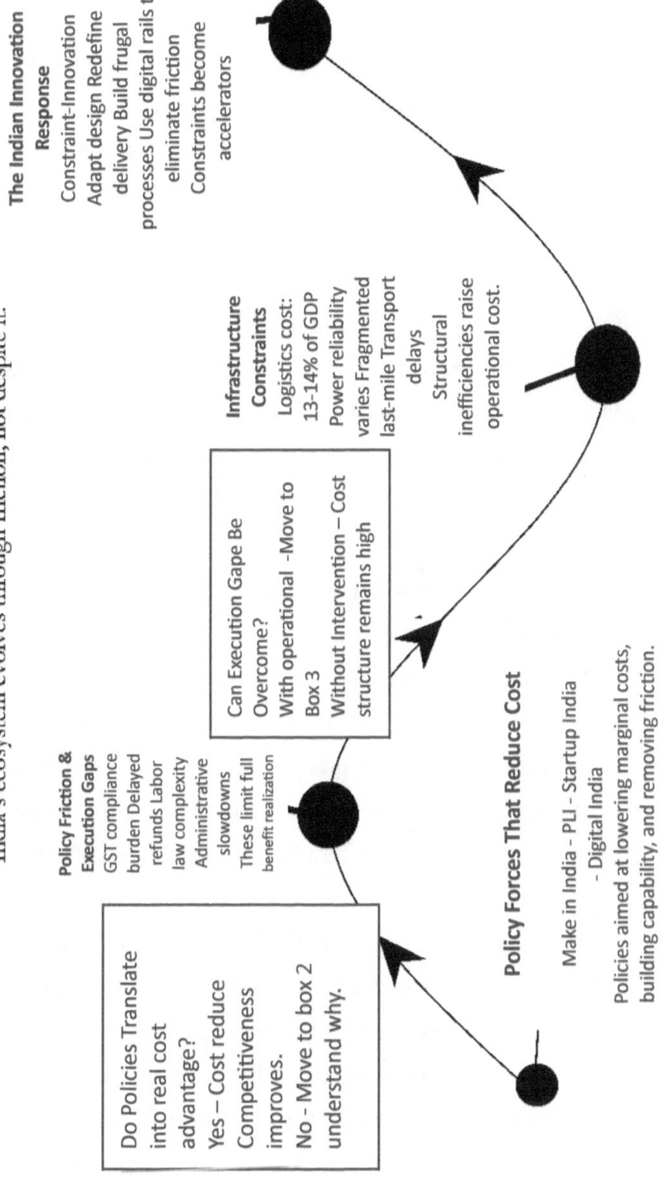

Therefore, successfully competing in India presents both opportunities and challenges for business leaders. Business leaders must view the political landscape as a key variable in formulating their competitive strategies.

Inefficiencies in logistics will cause companies to use AI for route optimization, to explore multi-modal supply chains, to consider electrically powered delivery vehicles and trucks, to employ predictive maintenance technology, and to establish micro-warehouses instead of large warehouses. Energy constraints are driving the adoption of solar energy, microgrids, and energy-efficiency programs. At the same time, last-mile delivery challenges have pushed Indian businesses to partner with local networks, kiranas, community-based delivery systems, and gig workers. Contrary to common belief, the constraints do not constrain India; instead, they serve to rewire India's business model.

Resourcefulness (also known as Jugaad), Resilience, and Adaptability

Whenever I meet with global business leaders to discuss the Indian business landscape, one thing I often share that surprises them is that India has a much greater competitive advantage through its cultural approach, rather than via structural means. India's advantages have come from an attitude rather than policy, markets, or numbers.

Jugaad

The meaning of Jugaad in the West is usually taken out of context, viewed as a quality-compromising shortcut or an easier route. However, Juguad represents the best example of resourceful, creative problem-solving. For example, I have witnessed numerous cases in which teams from various small machine shops create different configurations of implemented tools to maintain the production line.

On another occasion, I have also seen rural entrepreneurs adapt machinery to meet particular regional needs. Additionally, I have witnessed small logistics teams innovate with less than $1000 in their operations. What must be remembered in conjunction with the definition of Jugaad is that jugaad must have structure. The minute one starts cutting corners for the sake of frugality, you lose value. When we marry frugality with rational thought and manufacturing engineering perfection, we succeed.

India's Natural Resilience

Resilience is one of the defining characteristics of Indian culture. Growing up in India shapes your ability to deal with uncertainty, scarcity, diversity, and complexity. The Indian business community has demonstrated time and time again that, when faced with changing policies, a sudden increase in supply, or the ebb and flow of market demand, they do not panic but instead take the necessary steps to address the situation. I have seen teams completely transform their operational procedures in less than a week. I have seen entire distribution chains adjusted in a matter of hours. I have seen people in frontline organizations remain calm and collected under pressure, despite having spent their entire lives in a world of domestic unpredictability and insecurity. Resilience is not a business strategy; it is a necessity for survival.

Family-Led Trust and Professionalization

Family-owned, trusted Companies and Family-Run Companies have become accustomed to adding extra dimensions to their businesses:

- Building and maintaining a long-term, trust-based relationship;

- Encouraging investment by being more frugal than most other businesses, and
- Providing opportunity to generations beyond the first.
- Strong emotional commitment to customers and communities.

The shift we see today, where family governance blends with professional management, is creating hybrid organizations that possess the emotional intelligence of a family firm and the operational rigor of a corporation.

When you add frugality, resilience, and continuity together, you get one of India's biggest competitive strengths: the ability to adapt without losing identity.

Global Lessons from Indian Playbooks

Whenever I look at Indian companies succeeding globally, I see a pattern: they take the very capabilities they built to survive in India, cost discipline, frugal innovation, trust-based scaling, and apply them to international markets with remarkable success.

The Process of Reverse Exporting Frugal Production

While we often hear of the concept of "Making in India", we are beginning to recognize that a far more significant concept is "Making for India becomes Making for the World".

The technologies and products that India is creating by accounting for the specific constraints of price sensitivity, access to infrastructure, and diverse customer types will often work even better in many other emerging markets around the globe, such as Africa, Southeast Asia, and Latin America.

The reason these products are successful in other markets is that they still meet the need for high priority and low-cost tolerance, even with inconsistent infrastructure.

Indian Companies Succeeding Internationally

Tata Motors manages the iconic brand JLR and delivers value to its customers. Mahindra has created durable products that provide great value and are sold successfully in many rural areas around the world. Amul's cooperative business model is successful in providing consumers with world-class dairy products. Indian Pharmaceuticals has become a world leader in the generic pharmaceutical marketplace by providing high-quality products at competitive prices. Indian companies have been successful in the international marketplace not by duplicating the business models of their Western competitors, but by exporting the logic of Indian business practices and the innovations developed to address the challenges of the Indian domestic market.

The Winning Formula

The best Indian playbooks share three foundational traits: Design for value, not indulgence. Scale with trust and distribution depth. Utilize digital tools to compress costs and expand reach. India's business DNA is becoming a global competitive advantage. The world is learning from models we created out of necessity.

India as a Testing Ground for Innovation Models		
When Global Companies Misread India	India Rewards Companies That Listen First	The India Advantage for Innovation
There's a long list of global brands that entered India confidently and exited quietly.	On the other end, I've seen healthcare startups thrive by using local clinics as diagnostic hubs, combining low-	India forces organizations to: • simplify offerings, • Redesign cost structures,

Many assumed that Western value perception would translate directly. It didn't. Walmart faced challenges in understanding local consumption habits and the realities of distribution: Kellogg's misjudged taste, breakfast behavior, and price sensitivity. Several premium FMCG brands entered the market with global strategies, but failed because they lacked regional adaptation. These failures weren't about product quality. They were about context blindness.	cost technology with trusted neighborhood interfaces. I've seen consumer electronics companies scale nationally by stripping out "nice-to-have" features while doubling the number of after-sales service touchpoints, because reliability mattered more than specifications. In every example, the winners were those who asked, "What does India really value?" And then designed backwards from that answer.	• Innovate for uneven infrastructure, • Adapt to cultural diversity, • Build trust-based delivery models, • And use digital to compress costs and expand reach. This makes India a natural proving ground for innovation, not the kind built in labs, but the kind that survives in dynamic, demanding, high-volume markets.
If you build for India, you're not just building for a country; you're building for a nation. You're building for the future of cost-value markets worldwide.		

Leadership Mindset to Compete in India

When working with leadership teams based in India, I often remind them that they cannot be successful in India using an old mindset; they may not use legacy feeds, static playbook guides, or strategies built for predictable environments. Leadership in India will require speed, compassion, contextual awareness, and a willingness to enter the market with a learning mindset.

Rethink Your Organization

Many organizations were founded decades ago and continue to use organizational structures created for a slower-paced environment, along with the same processes and systems, including outdated technology and paperwork-driven approvals. However, in today's world, India does not wait for others to take advantage of the opportunities presented by technological and consumer behavior changes. Consumers, competition, and the marketplace itself are moving at the speed of light. I have told many business leaders that "your biggest problem isn't the market; it is the internal max speed limit you've created". For a business in India to be successful, leadership must enable the workforce to innovate, adapt culturally, and transform operations digitally.

Profitability with an End-to-End Mindset

The days of viewing profitability in isolation have ended for businesses in India. The P&L of a factory, a product line, or a market area means nothing without an overall understanding of the customer's profitability. What customer(s) are profitable? Which customer segments are costing businesses the most? Which product channels have hidden costs? In India's high volume/low margin environment, the leader's ability to understand the complexities of profitability will ultimately determine the survival of any business."

Future-Ready Decisions and Growth Mindset

The best competitors in India recognize the value of operating on 3- to 5-year timeframes rather than on quarterly or campaign timeframes. They typically invest in developing their capabilities before there is enough demand for those capabilities; they design for scale before that opportunity arises; they use digital technology before it becomes a necessity for everyone. Winning the business in India will require leaders who can navigate current limitations while remaining focused on future growth. It is a combination of practical consideration and visionary thinking.

India is a masterclass in strategic adaptability. If I had to distill this chapter into a few essential lessons, they would be these:

- In India, the markets cannot be stereotyped as one single market. Any strategy that treats India as a single and uniform market is sure to fail.

- Frugality is not an alternative to competition or advantage but rather a strategic asset, particularly when used in conjunction with precise engineering and digital leverage.

- Trust is an asset. Several factors influence customers' perceptions of trustworthiness more than product features alone, such as accessibility, after-sales service, and reliability.

- The informal economy in India is the hidden engine of the economy - agile and innovative but closely connected to local market conditions.

- Digital India has changed the cost equation for businesses. With the advent of UPI, Aadhaar, and mobile-first behavior, companies can add scale without experiencing a corresponding increase in costs.

- Policies and India's infrastructure create a foundation that can confer competitive advantages or disadvantages on any given business. The leaders in India must treat these variables as strategic; they are not simply externalities for business.

- The process of designing a product in India prepares you for selling it in other parts of the world. The frugal, scalable, trust-driven products created in India will be easily adapted to the world's emerging markets.

India rewards leaders who think with clarity, act with speed, and innovate with empathy.

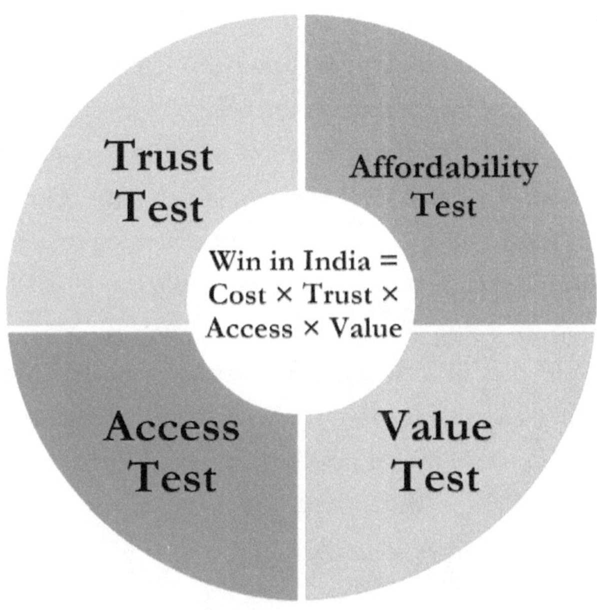

India Market Value-Cost Tests

Before continuing, I would like you to take a moment to pause and to apply an 'India lens' to your business. Do not view this as an academic exercise; view it instead as the first step in conducting a strategic reset of your business thinking.

Start by asking yourself, 'Am I thinking that premium = value?'

This assumption does not hold for India – a country where what we consider 'value' is defined by emotions, functionality, and context. You should then select one product, service, or delivery method from your portfolio and apply the four tests to determine whether it aligns with the three key principles of emotional, functional, and contextual value.

Next, identify one assumption you've always held about the Indian market and challenge it.

- Maybe it's pricing.
- Maybe it's the distribution.
- Maybe it's the type of customer you serve.
- Maybe it's the features you believe are essential.

Finally, redesign that assumption using India's winning equation: More value. Less cost. Zero compromise on trust. This is how you convert insight into action. In India, the winning strategy is neither low cost nor premium positioning-it is intelligent value delivered with precision.

I said that India is not a market; it's a mosaic. After walking through its cultural layers, digital rails, informal engines, and policy shifts, the picture should now be clear: India doesn't just challenge businesses, it shapes better ones.

Chapter 6
Technology as a Force Multiplier

In the last 10 years, I've seen technology many times does not fix what people do: it makes what people want to do bigger and clearer, but it does nothing to influence how well they accomplish their goals. It is possible to have a machine with all the latest gadgets that measure how much you're using, but if you're not monitoring the displays, it is useless. I have walked into factories where all employees were using the most advanced machines available, but they had never looked at their dashboards or tracks. I've met with sales teams using CRMs (Customer relationship management) and received hundreds of emails each month, but I've failed to manage their relationships or sales activities via the CRMs because they use WhatsApp. I have also seen companies spend millions on ERPs (Enterprise Resource Planning) or other accounting systems and use paper slips for purchase approvals.

And then I've also seen the opposite: a mid-sized company using a simple workflow tool to significantly reduce its turnaround time. A logistics firm is using geo-tagging to reduce idle time, and a plant is applying real-time monitoring to cut defects.

Same country. Same cost pressures. Same technology categories. The difference was not the tools; it was clarity.

Most organizations mistakenly believe that technology alone can meet their transformational needs. Technology doesn't create anything; instead, it provides a means for getting there. It only increases whatever is already there.

If a company has poor processes, technology will magnify those defects. If a company has an unclear organizational culture, technology will only make that confusion more evident. If a company has a weak or unclear strategy, its technology use will reveal that weakness to multiple customers.

On the other hand, when teams have clarity about what they want to achieve, the problems they need to solve, and the outcomes that matter, technology becomes a force multiplier. It speeds up decisions. It removes friction. It unlocks scalability. It provides leaders with real-time visibility, rather than relying on educated guesses.

This chapter is about that difference. Not technology for its own sake, not dashboards for decoration, not transformation as a vanity project, but technology as a strategic enabler of cost competitiveness and value creation.

Because when used with purpose, technology allows you to do something extraordinary: Deliver higher precision at lower cost, and create deeper value with fewer resources. And that is where the real power lies.

Technology as a Strategic Multiplier

When I talk about technology as a "force multiplier," I'm not referring to shiny tools, massive IT budgets, or complicated architectures. I'm talking about something far simpler and far more profound: technology becomes transformative only when it aligns with strategy and culture.

Technology alone will not create differentiation. You will purchase the same software, sign up for the same cloud platform, and deploy the same AI models as your competitors.

The key to gaining an advantage over your competition is how you use those products and services: whether you treat them as ancillary or have made them part of your business's fundamental way of thinking and operating.

I've encountered businesses that employ products merely because "competitors are adopting it," because a vendor convinced them, or just because it seems like the newest thing to do. That's how you lose money, consistency, and confidence in your digital investments.

On the contrary, when technology aligns with business outcomes, the situation is entirely different: less downtime, quicker turnaround, better customer retention, fewer defects, and greater capacity utilization. All of a sudden, dashboards are helpful—automation matters. AI understands. Data is a decision-making instrument, not a decorative element.

What Technology Brings to the Table

Technology creates impact in three fundamental ways: visibility, speed, and consistency. Everything else, AI, automation, IoT, analytics, all lead back to these three pillars.

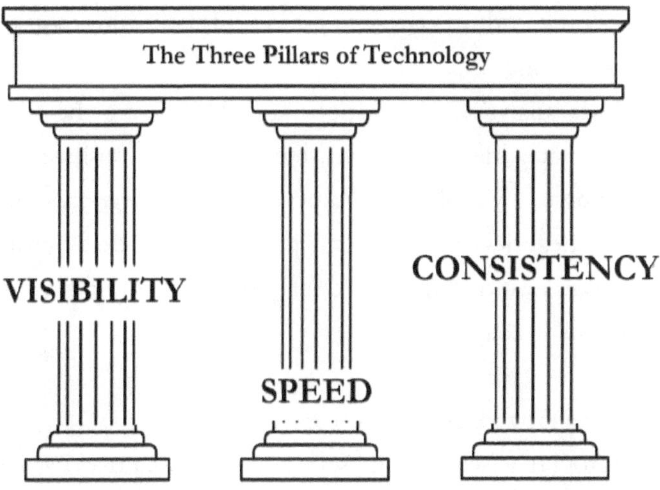

I've been to meetings where different departments used different data sets and interpretations. Clarity, accountability, transparency, and improved decision-making can be achieved through technology such as integrated ERP, CRM, and real-time dashboards. Reducing costs associated with hesitation and taking action based on real-time data are key components of speed. Automation eliminates low-value jobs, allowing knowledge, experience, and empathy to be prioritized rather than replacing people. Technology by itself only draws attention to problems rather than solving unclear or inefficient procedures. Redesign procedures and establish specific objectives before using technology. To reap the benefits of tools, adopt a technology-first strategy that is clear, well-designed, and aligned with the corporate culture.

Digital Transformation and Cost-Value Impact

When people hear the term "digital transformation," they often think of huge IT investments, complex architectures, and multi-year programs. The reality is much simpler: digital transformation is only valuable if it improves cost structures while increasing customer value. All else is noise.

Data analytics, automation, and AI/ML are the three digital impact categories that consistently deliver positive outcomes, according to my professional experience across a variety of industries. These categories are more than just catchphrases; by changing the cost-value relationship, they offer a practical way for a business to achieve its strategic objectives.

Data Analytics

A tool that helps businesses set competitive prices by giving them insight into their actual expenses. You cannot effectively control your expenses if you cannot see the actual cost of rendering a service. During my time working in manufacturing facilities, I discovered that the leadership teams of these companies relied on estimates rather than actual measurements because they were ignorant of their proper cost drivers, such as production machinery downtime due to maintenance issues, energy waste, rework rates, or procurement cost inefficiencies.

However, when data is available and is actionable, all of that will change. I have seen teams perform a complete job from gut feel to accuracy with systems such as activity-based costing, granular P&Ls, and earned value management (EVM). The minute they could see:

- Where the money was leaking,
- Where there were process leaks,
- Where the breaking points were,

They went from strategic decision-making to reactionary decision-making. One manufacturing team used a simple captive tool to achieve an astounding level of accuracy in tracking schedule and cost variances. Within weeks, they accurately predicted and reduced cost overruns, all without incurring any analytics-related expenses. Data-driven transformation doesn't require sophistication. It requires clarity.

Automation

Most repetitive tasks in a company can be automated. Employees' employment is not taken away by automation; instead, the friction involved in these operations is eliminated. I've previously witnessed companies automate:

- Quality Assessments
- Workflow Permissions
- Managing Materials

- Processing of Invoices
- Scheduling of Production

A team that used an automation tool and saved about two hours of reporting time each day is an example of this.

By digitizing its checklists, one factory also decreased errors made during manual inspections. It makes obvious sense: you allow people to concentrate on judgment, creativity, and customer service by relieving them of tedious, repetitive tasks. Automation lowers expenses by:

- Reducing Error Rates
- Cutting Cycle Time
- Boosting Uptime
- Increasing Consistency, Quality, and Reliability

AI and ML

The transition from responding to predicting is one of the most significant changes I have observed. Thanks to AI and ML capabilities, businesses can now identify potential problems before they become issues. Tata Steel used digital twins and predictive models to proactively manage maintenance.

They were able to reduce unplanned downtime, enhance production schedules, and foresee equipment breakdowns as a result. These developments have had a significant impact on the price.

In a similar vein, demand forecasting powered by AI increases inventory accuracy. Personalization engines enhance customer retention. Quality problems can be detected by machine learning models faster than by human inspection. AI is the present capability and future differentiator. It is no longer a technology initiative; it is a business imperative.

The Internet of Things (IoT)

The Internet of Things (IoT) allows for bringing together the physical aspects of our daily lives with the electronic aspects of the items themselves. Sensors, connectivity, and dashboards help our companies make decisions based on real-time information rather than relying solely on yesterday's data. In India, I have witnessed that using IoT to change the way we operate can even surprise very experienced leaders. For example, Indian Oil is currently using IoT to monitor pipes and identify leaks, saving money. The company that transports temperature-sensitive goods used IoT to track shipments, reducing spoilage and waste. Companies such as Infosys have also applied IoT and sensor analytics to help lower energy costs in their data centers.

Blind spots are eliminated through the deployment of IoT technologies in these industries. Eliminating blind spots means eliminating waste.

Using Technology to Create a Continuous Cycle of Cost and Value.

Gather leads to Analyze, cause your analysis to Act, and Optimize the act. This is the basic premise of digital transformation - not some grand strategy. It does not require a significant investment—just focused, incremental improvement driven by data and technology. Digital transformation is not a tool - it is the capacity to use digital to drive ongoing cost-value impact.

Creating a Digital Ecosystem Based on Value

When organizations discuss digital transformation, they frequently focus on tools such as ERP, CRM, cloud computing, AI, and analytics. However, tools alone do not create an advantage. Ecosystems do.

The Value-Centric Digital Ecosystem

- Data
- Insight
- Processes
- Technology
- Governance

A value-focused digital ecosystem unites all of your company's components, people, data, processes, and decision-making under the single objective of delivering value to clients while cutting expenses.

The Role of Digital Initiatives in Realizing Your Strategic Goals

What strategic objectives they will assist you in achieving should be the primary focus of all digital activities. Will it spur expansion? Boost profit margins? Cut expenses? Boost client retention? Increase uptime? Boost worker output? A digital project is more likely to be a waste of money if it is not precisely aligned with one or more of your strategic objectives.

Using carefully chosen technologies that complement its goal, Tata Motors' EV ecosystem plan is an excellent example of building a digital backbone to enable dependable products, predictable service, and a customer experience. A value-centric model is the end product.

Cross-Functional Integration

Technology must serve all purposes holistically rather than creating islands. When sales utilize CRM and the supply chain employs spreadsheets, data becomes scattered. When operations and finance use distinct metrics, decision-making conflicts arise.

Manufacturing does not change when HR uses digital technology; culture does. Businesses that have unified data spines—one customer record, one supply chain view, one financial reality, and one operation's heartbeat—are the most competitive.

This is what companies like Unilever achieved with their global data lakes. This is how Tesla and P&G run real-time control towers. And this is precisely what Indian companies must replicate in their own context.

Assessing ROI

Since technology ROI must be evaluated using a cost-value-impact equation, you shouldn't gauge ROI solely in terms of rupees saved or licenses activated:

- **Cost:** decreased downtime, automation ROI, and unit cost reduction.
- **Value:** stickiness, smoothness, and client happiness.
- **Impact:** increases in productivity, decision-making accuracy, and execution speed.

Risks of Tech Without Cultural Readiness

An unprepared culture was the primary cause of every unsuccessful digital transition I've witnessed. Not a shortage of funds. Not a deficiency of equipment. Not a lack of skill. It's simply a mismatch between cultural aptitude and technological desire.

- **Tool-First or Strategy-First Failure:** Many businesses utilize tools because "the board wants digital," "competitors are doing it," "vendors guaranteed ROI," or "it seems modern." But when tools are used without a plan, pandemonium results. The bakery created more problems than it solved by installing an expensive robot without redesigning its operations. The business that overloaded SAP with modifications, making it unworkable. The instruments were successful. The strategy didn't work.

- **Digital Fatigue**: I've walked into organizations where employees must log into multiple different systems to complete a day's work. Each tool makes sense on its own, but together they create a sense of exhaustion. Digital fatigue happens when:
  - tools exceed the capacity of users,
  - duplication replaces collaboration,
  - Complexity overwhelms purpose.

  This is the "illusion of progress": more tech, less productivity.

- **Cultural Misalignment:** Technology makes people more visible. Accountability is increased by visibility. Additionally, accountability fosters resistance if it is not culturally embraced. Because the transparency reveals inefficiencies or entrenched power dynamics, frontline staff members occasionally undermine digital systems. This isn't because humans are fundamentally flawed; instead, it's because society wasn't in sync before the introduction of technology.

- **Strategy Before Tools, Culture Before Tech**: Digital transformation works when:
  - People understand the "why",
  - There are overhauled processes,
  - Leadership is modeling the behavior, and
  - The absence of fear empowers teams.

Technology is powerful. Without cultural readiness, it's an expensive diversion.

Strategic Adoption & Scaling

My response is always the same when asked how businesses should start their digital journey: start small, learn quickly, and scale purposefully. When businesses attempt to deploy everything at once, digital transformation fails. When they experiment with clarity, based on actual challenges, it succeeds.

Coherence is more critical in strategic adoption than rapidity. The

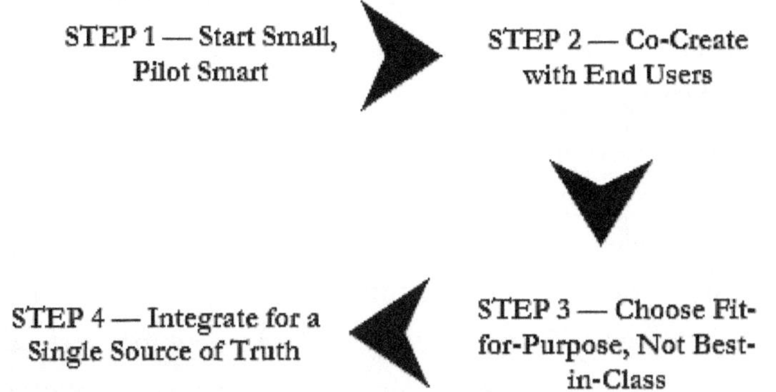

most obvious proof of what technology can accomplish when used purposefully is frequently found in case studies. These are a handful that stuck with me. Once, a mid-sized Indian business made a significant investment in a CRM system.

Their informal, relationship-driven, and unstructured sales process was the issue, not the CRM. Sales representatives didn't use the system because they were required to log 20 fields following each visit.

CRM was reduced to the three most important indicators: conversion probability, opportunity size, and visit frequency. Usage increased dramatically. Forecasting became more accurate. The velocity of sales rose. Clarity, not technology, altered the society.

In another case, a logistics company faced rising fuel costs, idle time, and inconsistent driver behavior. They installed geo-tagging and route analytics, which provided added visibility into what was happening in real time. By simply tweaking its operations in line with that information, the company significantly reduced turnaround time.

As a notable example, Tata Steel transformed the use of digital twins and predictive maintenance. The system would alert at the moment a breakdown occurs, allowing them to take action to prevent it. Achieving:

- fewer unplanned stoppages,
- lower cost of repair,
- higher overall asset utilization,
- better quality consistency.

This is what digital excellence looks like, applied to real industrial pain points. Indian Oil implemented real-time monitoring to detect two key indicators: pressure anomalies and leaks.

With stretch pipelines spanning great distances, even a minor leak can cause significant economic and environmental havoc. Real-time industrial IoT has saved crores from potential losses. Similarly, one retail company integrated its online and offline data to connect inventory and customer history. The customer had a seamless purchasing experience, and the company had accurate forecasts. Sales increased without additional marketing expenditures. The lesson in each story is simple: technology succeeds when it solves real problems, not when it decorates presentations.

Using Technology to Amplify Value Creation

Old View of Technology	New View of Technology (Value Multiplier)
Automation reduces headcount	Automation frees people for higher-value work.
Dashboards reduce reporting effort.	Dashboards improve visibility and decision speed.
ERP reduces paperwork	ERP enhances integration, accuracy, and scalability
Technology is seen mainly as a cost-cutting tool	Technology is seen as a growth, value, and capability amplifier

Technology-Enabled Value Drivers

Value Driver	How Technology Creates Value (Not Just Savings)	Outcome
Personalization at Scale	AI/ML-based personalization strengthens relevance and engagement	Higher retention & higher lifetime value
Platforms & Subscriptions	Digital platforms, subscription models, usage-based models	More predictable revenue, deeper customer stickiness
Speed as a Value Driver	Faster product development, quicker service delivery, and real-time response systems	Market advantage through speed, not price

Metrics Leaders Should Track

Only when we measure technology through the appropriate lenses does it have an impact.

You will feel busy but accomplish nothing if you focus on vanity metrics like the number of dashboards created, tools installed, or licenses acquired. I've witnessed businesses laud "digital adoption" in the absence of any change in business results. That is an illusion, not a transformation.

Only when leaders combine cost, value, and effect will the true power of technology become apparent.

Cost Efficiency Metrics	Value Creation Metrics	Operational Precision Metrics	Future -Readiness Metrics
Unit cost of production or service Automation ROI Energy cost per unit Cost per transaction or ticket	NPS (Net Promoter Score) Customer retention rate Revenue per customer Cost per query/cost per resolution	Downtime Quality/yield Cycle time Forecast accuracy	Digital revenue share Automation coverage Innovation throughput ESG and sustainability indicators

Avoiding the Tech Hype Trap

I've seen far too many businesses use tools just because they're hot, falling into the hype trap. Blockchain. Metaverse. AI. Cloud. RPA. The board is under pressure to "do something digital" because of these buzzwords. However, technology is only noise without a problem description. "Which problem does this solve?" is the one question I usually ask clients who make grand transformation promises.

The tool is not needed if the response is ambiguous. There are three ways that the hype trap manifests:

- Purchasing before considering is known as "tool-first implementation."
- Selecting "best-in-class" tools that are inappropriate for the situation is known as "shiny object syndrome."

- Adopting technology that appears contemporary but makes no modifications is known as digital wallpaper.

Leaders must resist the temptation to chase trends. Technology should be fit for purpose, not fashionable. The goal is not to impress the boardroom; it is to enable the teams that carry the weight of daily execution.

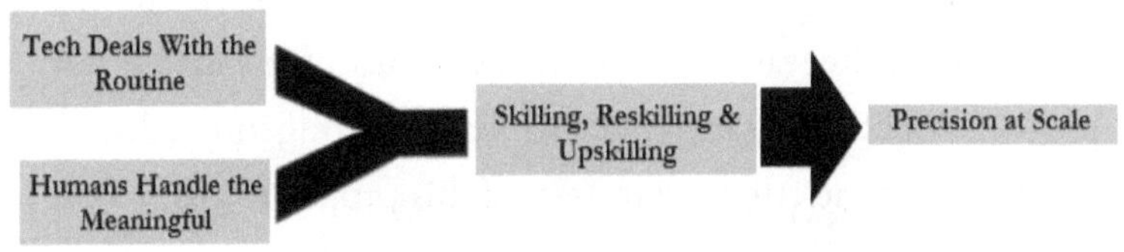

Human + Tech = Precision at Scale

Humans Plus Technology

For all the excitement around AI, automation, and digitalization, one truth remains unchanged: people create value, and technology amplifies it. I have witnessed organizations worry about positions being taken away from them by automation.

However, the truth is that automation will eliminate tasks, not people. Automation removes repetitive tasks, allowing humans to add more value by doing what they do best, such as problem-solving, empathizing with customers, building relationships, and thinking creatively. Technology becomes a competitive advantage only when it is intentionally designed, culturally embraced, and relentlessly measured.

Before moving forward, I would like you to conduct a simple, honest audit of your technology initiatives. This is not a technical exercise; it is a strategic reset. List your **top three technology investments** or projects. For each, ask these questions:

- Cost Competitiveness Test: Does this project lower unit costs, waste, downtime, error rates, or friction? The project lacks an economic basis if the answer is ambiguous.

- Customer Value Test: Does this technology improve, expedite, ease, or customize the customer's life? If not, you can be losing externally while optimizing internally.

- Strategic Alignment Test: Is this project related to capacity development, growth, retention, or margin improvement? Rethink it if it merely "modernizes" without changing metrics.

- Adoption Test: Are the tool's users engaged, knowledgeable, and in sync? A tool that is not in use is an expense rather than an asset.

Now, eliminate or redesign every initiative that fails these tests.

Finally, empower one team this month to pilot a value-aligned digital improvement. It could be:

- a workflow automation,
- a predictive alert system,
- a micro-dashboard for decision-making,
- an AI-based recommendation engine

Whatever creates a measurable cost-value impact. This is how transformation begins: one team, one problem, one purposeful solution.

What your company already has is enhanced by technology. Technology enhances your culture's emphasis on discipline, clarity, and customer-centric thinking. Technology exacerbates uncertainty if your teams work in silos, prevent openness, or oppose change.

This explains why many digital conversions don't work. The people weren't in sync, not because the technologies were flawed. Technology is not the future- it is the multiplier of the future.

Chapter 7
People, Culture, and Competitive Edge

Over the years, I've seen organizations invest millions in tools, systems, consultants, and processes, all in the hope of becoming more competitive. But the most powerful insight I've learned is this: your most significant source of cost advantage doesn't sit in a server room or a boardroom. It sits in your people.

Culture is not just a slogan on a wall or a paragraph in the annual report. It influences decision-making, especially when no one is watching. Recognizing this can empower leaders to shape behaviors under pressure and foster a resilient organization.

To understand a company's proper health, don't look solely at strategy decks. Instead, assess behaviors on the shop floor, in meetings, at the front desk, and in the field to identify cultural strengths and gaps that affect costs and performance.

Misalignment is one of the most hidden cost layers in any firm, as I have stated numerous times. Rework, delays, miscommunication, and friction can add crores of rupees in the form of people rowing in separate directions, departments operating with competing goals, or leaders sending inconsistent signals. Ironically, since these expenses aren't included in the P&L, most businesses aren't even aware of them. However, they are still very much present in the culture.

A culture of fear can be detrimental to a company's ability to innovate and grow. A culture of fear leads to employees who are less likely to speak up about issues that are occurring, share suggestions about ways to improve processes, or report any deficiencies, resulting in a situation where problems exist longer than they should, leading to delays in taking appropriate action and greater rework and costs than they otherwise would have incurred with timely intervention. What may first seem like a lack of enthusiasm for one's work may eventually lead to financial loss for the company. Most organizations that operate through fear, lose money, and incur costs because fear blocks innovation and creativity.

However, I have seen teams achieve remarkable outcomes when their leaders consciously create a culture of clarity, ownership, and psychological safety through focused efforts, employee training, and ongoing messaging. Employees will automatically cut waste, make suggestions for improvements, and maintain value when they feel appreciated, trusted, and empowered.

Thus, Culture is a Competitive Weapon. Culture helps keep an organization's costs down without compromising Dignity. Culture serves as the ultimate cost shield/engine and is the primary force behind all truly Competitive Companies.

The Culture is the Cost-Value Leadership Platform.

Culture acts as an invisible platform for how we operate as organizations; you can't see it but it runs everything (decisions, priorities, behaviors, trust/speed, ultimately cost etc.); while strategy will set the course, it will be culture that provides the means to execute; it is through this process of executing that we will (indirectly) affect our overall costs.

A company with a weak culture can have the best strategy in the world and still fail spectacularly. But give an average strategy to a team with a strong, aligned culture, and they will outperform their competitors with discipline, clarity, and relentless commitment.

Long-term value is based on an organization's culture, while short-term cost-cutting produces little value. When people have developed a cost-consciousness, a focus on precision, and a sense of ownership, they do not require reminders to save money or reduce waste; instead, they act automatically because it is the right thing to do. At this level of maturity, control of costs is a matter of belief, rather than compliance.

While supporting the organization's values of frugality and resource conservation may be the right thing to do, it may also meet with pushback due to past habits, mindsets, and attitudes. For organizations to shift this culture, leaders must consistently model the desired values, communicate openly and transparently about the desired behaviors, and reinforce them to integrate them into the culture.

A well-designed culture will remove friction, build trust, and facilitate alignment. On the other hand, a poorly designed culture creates hidden layers of cost due to miscommunication, confusion, and disconnection within the workforce, underscoring that culture should not be viewed as a soft, passive attribute; instead, it should be seen as a tangible, measurable business advantage.

If technology is the engine of competition in the modern world, then culture is the fuel for that engine. Without the right culture to support it, the best technological tools available today will not work optimally; however, even mid-range tools will produce optimal results when supported by a strong culture.

The Ultimate Cost Shield is Culture

Culture often sets the example for how an organization maintains control over costs or allows them to escalate out of control. The starting point for this Culture can come from an area of misalignment that many leaders overlook. Misalignment is where hidden costs emerge, not through ineffective strategies, but by having multiple departments working with conflicting objectives.

This kind of misalignment will cost the firm money, yet we have seen it happen again and again.

Finance was driven by quarterly savings rather than long-term profits; procurement focused on getting the best price without accounting for total expenses; and sales teams chased volume while operations sought stability. Even while each of these departments is doing remarkably well on its own, taken together, they result in cost leakage. Instead of failing drastically, organizations gradually lose value over time by continuing to optimize individual departmental measures at the expense of overall results.

Misalignments occur in our daily lives. For example, a poorly communicated change order will delay production for 2 weeks and ultimately cost several lakhs. An order requirement that was miscommunicated will create rework for the team, ultimately eroding capacity and morale. In addition, a single piece of missing information can lead to countless hours of wasted time due to unproductive conflict and lost decision-making time, as well as increased costs. None of the misalignments mentioned above is the result of operational failures; instead, they stem from a lack of cultural alignment amongst teams and are therefore failure experiences within team culture. Misalignments occur when teams do not share the same beliefs about their purpose, process, and priorities. Fear is the fundamental cause of failure. Silence brought on by fear results in decreased productivity. When employees are reluctant to discuss difficulties with their colleagues, issues go unreported until they escalate to a crisis. Excessive waste can emerge in a workplace when employees are afraid to question a defective procedure. Minor concerns can become major disruptions when frontline staff fail to escalate them out of fear of an adverse reaction. Fear discourages creativity and increases error rates.

When people are penalized for making errors more than they are rewarded for learning from them, employees won't share fresh ideas.

Additionally, companies with strong cultures are better at defending against unnecessary expenses than those with weak cultures. Workers in these settings are transparent in their communication, frequently reveal waste, and express concerns before the costs become too great. Teams function cooperatively, without ego, and with shared accountability. Teams reduce rework, make decisions more quickly, shorten time-to-value, and enhance customer satisfaction by aligning closely with the company culture. Even if some of these advancements won't show up immediately on the balance sheet, compounding will eventually provide them a sizable competitive advantage. Nokia's case is even more revealing. It wasn't technology that failed; it was leadership culture. Fear prevented teams from sharing critical truths. The result was catastrophic.

GE, once a global benchmark, fell into a trap of internal competition that rewarded politics over collaboration. Information hoarding, unrealistic commitments, and over-optimism created a layer upon layer of hidden costs, all of which were cultural in nature.

The conclusion drawn from these examples is that culture is either the most potent weapon against rising costs or quietly contributes to their escalation. A culture of alignment in cost optimization is a way of life rather than just a project.

The Development of Precision as an Action

The single most important belief I have come to understand is that precision is an action, rather than a tool.

A culture of precision does not appear in boardrooms and audits; instead, it develops within the small, consistent actions that solve problems before they manifest.

Precision Thinking = Invisible Cost Control	
When people think precisely, they work precisely. Precision thinking reduces rework, prevents miscommunication, and eliminates invisible waste. Clarity in decisions, communication, and action becomes an organization's most underestimated cost-saving tool.	
What Precision Thinking Eliminates	**What Precision Thinking Builds**
✗ Vague communication that creates confusion ✗ Escalations without context ✗ Commitments made without feasibility checks ✗ Improvised responses to customers	✓ Clarity in asking ✓ Clarity in documenting ✓ Clarity in committing ✓ Clarity in delivering

Everyday Behaviors		
• Notebook icon → *Clear communication & minutes*		
• Calendar icon → *Pre-read discipline*		
• Checkmark loop icon → *Closing loops*		
• Magnifying glass icon → *Fact-checking*		
• Puzzle icon → *Structured problem statements*		
• Folder icon → *Consistent documentation*		

Rituals That Reinforce Precision		
Daily Stand-ups	**Friday Data Integrity Checks**	**Retrospectives/ Post-Mortems**
What must I deliver? What is blocking me? What needs clarity?	Correct data early → prevent expensive downstream errors.	Where did we lose clarity? What assumption was wrong? What signal was missed?

> ### *Storytelling*
>
> *Stories make precision memorable. Narratives of people who prevented defects, clarified customer requirements, or solved problems through disciplined communication become cultural anchors.*

When Leaders Change, Culture Changes

Cultures are transformed by leaders changing how they lead. Employees don't follow the values in print; they follow what they observe being modeled.

Leader's Actions Provide the Model for Others to Follow

To create a culture of accuracy, leaders must communicate clearly. To develop a culture of economic efficiency, leaders must practice cost-sensitivity. To create a culture of personal and collective accountability, leaders must be accountable. The "fluff and stuff" type of leadership (those who appear busy for the sake of appearing busy, those who conduct numerous meetings but do not offer any actual value to the meetings, and those who create a sense of urgency without defining what that urgency is) adds to the noise but does not advance results. Leaders must demonstrate the behaviors they want multiplied, like showing up on time, closing commitments, asking value-driven questions, focusing on data, encouraging truth-telling, celebrating initiative, etc. Teams copy what leaders normalize.

Trust plus Toughness equals High-Performance Culture.

Cost pressure often pushes leaders into one of two extremes: either becoming too soft or too authoritarian. Both are dangerous. What high-performing cultures need instead is a balance: toughness in standards and softness in relationships.

- Tough on waste.
- Tough on excuses.

- Tough on clarity.
- Soft on people.
- Soft on learning.
- Soft on mistakes made in the pursuit of improvement.

Managing the tension between performance pressure and psychological safety. Without psychological safety, people tend to hide their problems. Without performance pressure, people don't grow.

Rewarding Long-Term Thinking, Not Short-Term Cuts

Instead of encouraging their teams to add value to consumers, many executives encourage them to cut costs. This could be detrimental, as short-term cost-cutting measures can undermine long-term capacity. Team members who exhibit customer obsession, accuracy, initiative, teamwork, learning, creativity, and ownership should be rewarded by their leaders. The organization's culture is strengthened when leaders' incentives align with long-term competitiveness.

When COVID-19 hit, many organizations reacted in a state of panic, implementing cost-cutting programs, fear-based controls, or suspending operations altogether; whereas some leaders took a different approach. I am aware of a situation where leadership at one organization continued to provide bonuses to employees for their outstanding performance even during a year of substantial loss, thus demonstrating that it was not an act of financial generosity but rather an act of providing a culture-building strategy; therefore, the act itself developed more trust in the team than any speech could have done. We need to establish a culture that provides clarity and agility, allowing people to adapt rapidly to the crisis rather than collapse as the environment changes.

People-First Cultures Drive Performance

Some people think you need a harsh management style to achieve cost-competitiveness. My experience has taught me differently, as greater efficiencies and lower overall operating costs result from a culture that values employees first.

One of the most potent elements in attaining cost-effective operations is employee engagement. People's involvement naturally rises when they feel valued, are part of something bigger, and are aware that their efforts have an impact. I frequently state that "the impacts of disengagement multiply," implying that a single disengaged worker can sap the vitality of many others. Conversely, if an employee is fully engaged, they can amplify the culture through their actions and multiply performance. For these reasons, the methods of achieving training, inclusion, and providing employees with independence should be treated as an investment in the company's future rather than simply as an expense. This is because well-trained individuals make fewer errors, employees who feel included are more engaged and respond more quickly to issues that may arise, and teams achieve quicker solutions when they feel empowered to make decisions with autonomy. There are simple ways to facilitate employee ownership of their careers through blind-room simulations. By allowing teams to feel a sense of ownership and to build deeper relationships and respect for one another, this fosters greater collaboration across departments, leading to higher productivity and fewer problems.

Of course, autonomy will be more effective when supported by proper company governance. The combination of giving employees the ability to act within their chosen areas of expertise with a clear sense of purpose and structure leads to faster, more accurate results.

Psychological safety also plays a decisive role. When employees feel safe reporting problems, sharing ideas, experimenting, and collaborating across functions, issues are caught earlier—and early detection is the cheapest form of cost control.

Most importantly, people feel empowered and create value through substantial discretionary effort because of the respect they receive from leaders. I have witnessed a shop-floor team with minimal resources achieving tremendous results simply because they were treated with dignity by their leaders. When an individual feels respected, their discretionary effort increases exponentially. Discretionary effort may not always be quantifiable, but it is one of the most effective ways to create sustainable cost benefits.

A people-first culture does not coddle or baby employees; it empowers them to perform at their highest levels. They view employees as individuals who contribute positively to the company rather than as costs. This shift in thinking is a greater contributor to performance improvements than any methodology or method ever created.

Alignment Driven by Stories

There's one cultural lever I trust more than all others – that is storytelling. While strategies can inform, stories can transform. Stories move faster than any strategy, stay in consumers' minds longer than strategies do, and help shape cultures more deeply than any PowerPoint presentation can.

The most significant cultural shifts I've seen were driven by stories about small, simple things done by normal people that encapsulated the message behind Precision, a Culture of Ownership, and a Culture of Customer Obsession. A factory supervisor taking action to reposition one item in the package, saving the organization significantly in shipping expenses is a story of the action taken was so widely shared that it became known as the story of an individual who had taken the initiative, driven by curiosity and a need for value-driven thinking. As a result, the opportunity for innovation was no longer limited to R&D; it was available to anyone with the desire and ability to take appropriate actions to drive improvement.

When we share stories of ordinary people doing extraordinary things, culture becomes a universal concept.

Organizations need to establish a sense of value and meaningful intent among employees. Employees derive this feeling from internal narrative foundations based upon their organization's experience as it applies to the following types of experiences: "This is what we do for customers," "This is how we solve a problem," "This is what we will do when we are faced with a problem," "This is how staff members create ideas," "This is how staff members display ownership." A team engaged in the "value-reflection" practice, in which each member shared one way they created value each week. As this practice evolved, it became part of the team's culture, serving as a mirror that helped individuals see themselves differently within the team. Stories are the voice of a culture.

Once a tale is conveyed, it becomes information. A cultural phenomenon is a narrative that has been told a hundred times. Leaders reinforce the organization's values and principles by consistently demonstrating thrift, accuracy, or customer-centricity. When the right actions are emphasized in public, they spread in private. An example of an unsuccessful cultural change project in which a team attempted to apply approaches for continuous improvement but presented them more as objectives than as learning opportunities.

The failure taught us that people don't embrace behaviors until they understand the "why," not just the "what." Failure stories can be powerful accelerators of alignment when told openly.

Culture in a Time of Change

Change does not disrupt culture, but it exposes it. In times of transformation or crisis, culture becomes most visible: how people behave under pressure.

The Value of Cultural Clarity in Development

Scaling serves as a stress test, demonstrating how businesses frequently lose consistency, clarity, and communication as they grow. Scaling can exacerbate cultural uncertainty, as I have long noted—roles become hazy, presumptions take root, and choices become subjective. Teams may adopt disparate definitions of "value" in the absence of established cultural standards, leading to undetected misalignment.

Handling Stress and Developing Resilience

A lack of emotional resilience might feel like overpowering terror, even when performance pressure is necessary for concentration. Fears stifles creativity, hides issues, and encourages taking short corners.

A resilient culture acknowledges both the pursuit of excellence and the protection of team members. Businesses that promote psychological safety before crises typically bounce back more quickly. These teams are better equipped to respond to challenges because they can review decisions, raise concerns early, and challenge presumptions.

Including New Talent in Cultural DNA

New talent adds diversity to organizations as they expand, but it also risks causing cultural drift. Leaders' ought to be thoughtful: clearly state expectations, describe the motivations behind significant behaviors, use rituals rather than merely procedures for onboarding, and tell tales of cultural role models. Cultural integration is about directing energies toward a shared goal, not about making everyone the same.

Culture Needs Active Protection, Not Assumption

Culture doesn't sustain itself. It requires daily nurturing, reinforcement, and protection, especially during times of change. If you don't intentionally shape culture during transformation, the process will shape you—sometimes in ways you might not want.

Culture is the invisible engine behind competitive advantage. When you build it intentionally, it pays back in every metric that matters: cost, quality, growth, resilience, and trust.

Please stop a moment and look at your culture from a different perspective, not as an observer but as a leader who is responsible for creating and shaping a culture. Ask yourself this question: Does your culture "silently enable cost leakage" or does it "actively support value creation"?

To answer this question honestly, consider the following two steps:

Step 1: Identify One Hidden Cost Due to Culture: Reflect on a recent situation where you experienced misalignment that slowed down a decision, unclear roles that led to rework, a lack of ownership that delayed a customer response, or you feared voicing a concern that allowed the problem to foster and grow. These issues are not just operational challenges; they represent cultural issues with high costs.

Step 2: Select One Specific Behavior That You Want to Foster This Week: Find a single habit, practice, mindset, or ritual that exemplifies both precision and purpose. An example could include a daily 10-minute stand-up meeting, a weekly meeting to assess the "value," a "no blame" post-mortem, or the habit of clarifying "what value looks like" before beginning any task. You do not need to launch a large-scale transformation effort to change your company's culture. You only need to identify one consistent behavior.

Step 3: Model It Relentlessly: Culture changes when leaders behave with intentionality. If you reinforce the habit consistently, publicly, and privately, others will follow.

When people see clarity, they build clarity. When they see ownership, they take ownership.

When they see value in thinking, they adopt it.

Your task this week is simple: **Choose one cultural behavior and anchor it in your team.** That single act can unlock a cascade of improvements in cost, quality, and customer experience.

You can invest in the best technology, the most sophisticated frameworks, or the most ambitious transformation programs. Still, none of them will deliver sustained impact if the culture underneath is fragile. Competitive edge is not built by the brilliance of a few but by the belief of many. People fuel execution; culture fuels persistence; together, they edge.

Culture is not an HR initiative. Culture is the operating system of the enterprise.

And when it is strong, everything else runs better: precision, performance, innovation, trust, and customer value.

Chapter 8
The Future-Ready Enterprise

I see a recurring pattern among businesses that fail during disruptive times: they are built to succeed in the upcoming quarter rather than the upcoming decade. Instead of rewarding long-term relevance, their systems prioritize short-term efficiency. Their leaders are more concerned with today's fires than with the future landscape. Additionally, in a world that is anything but predictable, their culture values predictability.

In contrast, the organizations that endure across industries, crises, and generations are built on a different mental model. They see volatility not as an anomaly but as a constant. They anticipate change before it arrives. They adapt before they are forced. They treat resilience and agility as strategic assets, not optional virtues.

I've seen this repeatedly. Companies with robust digital foundations were able to quickly and confidently survive COVID-19. Those that had strong supply chain visibility bounced back faster. Those who had engaged, empowered teams didn't freeze in fear. Those who had future-focused leaders didn't waste energy debating whether the world had changed; they accelerated into the new reality.

The future world will not be kind to those who seek certainty. It will be kind to those who prepare for uncertainty: climate change, geopolitical tensions, supply-chain reshaping, the acceleration of AI, changing regulations, and shifting demographics.

These are not unfounded future shocks; they are happening now, all of them in parallel. And they are impacting competitiveness in real time.

Being a future-ready company means you have planned for future developments rather than just responding to them. Organizations that are prepared for the future are flexible enough to change course, strong enough to withstand shocks, and imaginative enough to take the lead when others are reluctant. Organizations that are prepared for the future have developed the skills necessary to interact with it rather than merely waiting for it.

In this chapter, I will explore how organizations leverage adaptability into their DNA by designing systems, culture, and strategies that align cost, value, and long-term impact. Because the organizations that win tomorrow will not be the ones that accurately and favorably anticipate the future, they will be the ones with the organizational capacity to evolve dynamically, confidently, and intelligently.

If I had to summarize future-readiness in one sentence, it would be this: competitive advantage now comes from the ability to adapt faster than the environment changes. Traditional strategic planning was built on the assumption of stability. Today's strategy must be built on movement.

For years, competitiveness meant operational efficiency, cost control, standardization, and tight management. But efficiency alone can no longer keep a business relevant. Efficiency is retrospective. It optimizes for yesterday's reality.

Adaptability, on the other hand, prepares you for tomorrow.

Future-readiness isn't about predicting the next disruption; it is about building a mindset and system that can learn, adjust, and transform continuously. A future-ready enterprise aligns **cost**, **value**, and **impact** across three-time horizons:

- In the short term, it's about operational resilience and responsive speed.
- In the medium term, it's about innovation, digital transformation, and capability building.
- In the long term, it's about sustainability, purpose, and strategic foresight; and the glue between all these horizons is adaptability.

Redefining Competitiveness for the Future

Competitive advantage was once rewarded for efficiency, control, and predictability. The world is now different, and the old playbook is becoming less valuable. Today, competitive advantage is no longer measured by how well a company performs in ideal conditions, but rather by how effectively an organization adapts to ambiguous ones.

Despite the importance of efficiency, it is no longer the only factor to be considered. Agility, not certainty, is the new competitive advantage. This calls for a change in the movement from cost consciousness to value agility, which is the capacity to produce value even when the premises are challenged or even fall. Agility is demanding, as it implies being versatile in thinking, having flexible structures, and having trained teams that respond with clarity rather than fear. For years, companies have been using some fixed indicators to measure their competitiveness:

- Cost per unit
- Revenue growth
- Market share
- Operational effectiveness
- Return on investment

Those indicators are historical. They show the past, not the present. Organizations ready for the future are measuring their performance by very different indicators:

- Value delivered per cost unit
- Speed of learning and adapting
- Supply chain resilience
- Operational sustainability
- Customer lifetime impact
- Digital adaptability
- Culture health indicators

Today's organizations need to change their metrics from "how well did we perform" to "how ready are we." ESG (Environmental, Social, and Governance) was once viewed as a PR checkbox or a regulatory burden. That period of time has passed. ESG is currently redefining industry-wide competitiveness. Investors are rewarding sustainable businesses. Consumers are selecting ethical brands. Rules are becoming more stringent. Talent is drawn to companies with a clear mission. Value is not solely determined by money in the new competitiveness model. Impact on stakeholders, society, and the environment is used to gauge it. Businesses that are prepared for the future don't choose between purpose and profit. They create mutually reinforcing systems and, finally, deliver sustainability-adjusted cost leadership.

Designing for Adaptability

Looking back at the companies that have managed to exist and even grow during major disruptions, I can spot one thing in common: they were made to change. Not adding to it. Not merely a crisis coping measure. But definitely a principle of the organization's fabric.

Change is not a spur-of-the-moment thing; it's been planned and prepared. It is the deliberate creation of the learning-fast, acting-proactive, and responding-intentionally systems that make you wince.

Incorporating Agility into Strategy

The majority of organizations treat strategy as a fixed annual event, like a document created in calm conditions and rarely updated during storms. The enterprises that are ready for the future are not like this. They view the strategy as a living, breathing creature. They apply scenario planning to prepare for many different futures rather than just one. They create flexible structures so that growth will not make the organization rigid. And they delegate decision-making power, enabling people closest to the issue to respond right away without going through multiple layers of management for approval.

Decentralization of power is an essential factor. When leaders clearly give teams the authority with guidelines in place, companies can act more quickly while remaining aligned and consistent. During a crisis, companies that moved decision-making power to frontline teams had faster responses, fewer bottlenecks, and more people feeling responsible for the results. The more trust there is, the more flexibility there is, and vice versa.

Using Data for Anticipation, Not Just Insight

Every company today collects vast amounts of data. Very few use it to look ahead. Most dashboards describe what has already happened. Future-ready enterprises use data to sense early signals.

This means employing predictive analytics, customer behavior patterns, supply chain indicators, and key metrics that signal shifts before they become a crisis.

Moving from just data analysis to data forecasting, the company shifts from a reactive, firefighting approach to a proactive, outcomes-shaping approach.

Businesses that switched from monthly retrospective reporting to real-time predictive visibility could perform faster and with greater confidence. When your teams are aware of what is going to happen next, they become smarter and quicker in their response.

Learning Velocity as a Competitive Metric

One of the most overlooked metrics for the future is learning velocity, how fast your company absorbs new information, unlearns old assumptions, and develops new skills. Skill cycles are getting shorter. Market cycles are getting shorter. Customer expectations are getting higher. The companies that learn slowly will be left behind very quickly. Future-ready businesses are those that develop continuous learning systems, cross-functional exposure, experimentation budgets, rapid feedback loops, peer learning, digital skilling platforms, and reflective practices like retrospectives and post-mortems. The organizations that win tomorrow are learning organizations today.

Sustainability as Strategic Cost Discipline

A considerable number of executives continue to regard sustainability as an expense. Yet, it is the most potent method of cost discipline that can be put into practice in a firm. When your activi-ties are in harmony with nature, efficient in resource use, and guided by long-term thinking, you not only save the earth but also secure your financial well-being. Today, sustainability is one of the best ways to reduce operating costs in the long run. Companies that invest in energy-efficient equipment experience reduced operational costs.

Manufacturers enjoy higher profit margins by reducing waste. Transportation companies reduce pollution and incur lower fuel expenses by optimizing their routes.

This is the new formula: sustainable methods reduce leaks, inefficiencies, and unwanted surprises. Waste is costly. The cost of pollution is high. The cost of noncompliance is high. Anything that isn't sustainable eventually loses its profitability.

Simultaneously, firms that take accountability usually flourish. Today's companies see climate care as a competitive advantage rather than merely a CSR effort. More and more consumers are favoring brands that reflect their values. Skilled people are attracted to companies that prioritize social and environmental responsibility. Investors reward long-term ESG initiatives through lower capital costs and higher valuations. To mention a few, reduced material costs through green packaging, new revenue streams from circular models, and stronger ethical supply chains are examples of the hidden opportunity's companies discover when they regard sustainability as a business strategy rather than a moral obligation. The concepts of profitability and responsibility have become interdependent instead of opposing ones.

Businesses that are prepared for the future are broadening their concept of cost. They take into account something's planetary cost rather than just its financial cost. "What does this cost the environment?" they inquire. "What is the cost to society of this?" "In the long term, what will this cost our reputation?" Leaders may prevent today's decisions from becoming tomorrow's problems by internalizing these larger questions. It is strategic to consider the planetary cost rather than a utopian one. It helps businesses safeguard their future while boosting their current competitiveness.

Future-Readiness Frameworks

As I've worked with organizations across industries and continents, I've realized that the enterprises built for the future share a typical architecture. It isn't a technology stack. It isn't an industry secret. It's a disciplined blend of three capabilities that reinforce each other: Lean, Green, and Human.

This is the triad of future-readiness, a framework that enables companies to operate with efficiency, responsibility, and empathy simultaneously. When these three come together, cost competitiveness and value creation cease to be trade-offs and become reinforcing loops.

Lean	Green	Human
A future-ready company is operationally fit. It eliminates friction, minimizes waste, and uses data to inform decisions rather than relying on intuition to react. "Lean" doesn't mean cutting deeper every year. It means using resources deliberately, allocating effort where it has the most significant impact, not where habit or hierarchy dictates.	"Green" is no longer the ethical nice-to-have it once was. It is a strategic imperative. Companies that embed sustainability into their sourcing, manufacturing, distribution, and customer engagement processes create resilience that pure cost-cutting can never deliver Green practices strengthen compliance, reduce risk, improve brand	A future-ready enterprise is deeply human. It recognizes that resilience cannot be automated. Judgment cannot be outsourced. Creativity cannot be programmed. People are the real system. And culture is the operating logic. A "Human" organization builds psychological safety, celebrates learning, encourages dissent, and empowers ownership. It

Lean organizations run on clarity. Every team knows its role in delivering value, and every process has a purpose. When cost structures reflect priorities rather than legacy, the entire system becomes agile.	trust, and often unlock new revenue streams. They also protect companies from rising energy, material, and waste costs, as well as carbon regulations. Future-ready organizations recognize that planetary stability and business stability are inextricably linked.	invests in well-being, diversity, and long-term capability building. When people feel valued, they contribute value. When they feel safe, they take risks intelligently. When they feel connected to purpose, they go beyond KPIs.

Together, the Lean, Green, and Human model becomes a triad of sustainable competitiveness, efficient operations, responsible growth, and people-driven innovation, reinforcing each other continuously.

Multiple cases where companies transformed not by predicting the future, but by preparing for it. The thread that connects them is this: they used constraints as catalysts, culture as infrastructure, and clarity as a compass.

For many years, a multinational consumer brand saw ESG compliance as merely a regulatory checklist and a cumbersome necessity. Once they reframed it as a business opportunity, that changed. They mapped supplier sustainability data, used energy-efficient factories, and modified packaging to reduce plastic use. Over the course of three years, they reduced emissions, saved millions in material costs, and began securing contracts with major international retailers seeking ethical partners. ESG did not slow them down; it differentiated them.

A manufacturing company that experienced significant supply chain disruption during the COVID years. Instead of wholesale fixes to the existing model, they rewired it. They decentralized sourcing, emphasized local vendor development, and digitized procurement. As a result, you see a more resilient, flexible, and transparent system, one that reduces dependency, improves responsiveness, and lowers risk exposure.

I want to reference a small, legacy business that has been in existence for over a century, outlasting wars, recessions, political upheavals, and technological revolutions. Their secret to success? It wasn't tradition. It was evolution. Every decade, they took the time to assess their portfolio, renew their talent, and reconsider their purpose for a new generation of customers, leaving almost nothing untouched—excluding their underlying values. It was that combination of continuity and reinvention that has upheld their relevance today and their significance over the last century.

One thing is clear from these tales: being prepared for the future is leadership in slow motion, not luck. Redesigning before disruption compels you to do so; taking that on takes guts. In the world, there are two types of businesses. The ones quietly building for the next 10 years and those getting ready for the next quarter. They are not different in terms of size, cost, or location. It's a way of thinking. It's intentionality. It is the readiness to do more than endure the future.

Every tactic, system, and cultural change has one thing in common: leadership. The obligation, not the function. The awareness, not the authority. Future readiness isn't built by strategy alone, but by culture with agility. In the next decade, resilience will perform prediction.

Conclusion

As I look back on the ideas, stories, and experiences shared in this book, one truth stands out with unmistakable clarity: enduring winners are not built by optimizing parts, but by aligning the whole. The most competitive organizations do not treat cost as a finance problem, innovation as a creative exercise, culture as an HR responsibility, or technology as an IT project. They understand that competitiveness is a system—and leadership is the force that integrates it.

Across industries and decades, I have learned that the most formidable challenges rarely live inside spreadsheets. They live inside mindsets. They show up in how leaders interpret trade-offs, how teams respond to pressure, and how organizations choose clarity over comfort. Competitive advantage, therefore, does not emerge from isolated initiatives or heroic interventions. It emerges from coherence.

This book has been my attempt to offer leaders a way to build that coherence, not through rigid frameworks or one-size-fits-all prescriptions, but through a set of interdependent lenses—cost, value, precision, culture, innovation, technology, and future-readiness. Each lens matters on its own. Together, they shape how an organization thinks, decides, and acts. And that integrated way of operating is far more complex to replicate than any single strategy or tool.

If there is one idea I hope stays with you, it is this: excellence in isolation is fragile. Integration is durable. Leaders who can connect cost with value, discipline with innovation, technology with judgment, and today's decisions with tomorrow's consequences build organizations that do more than perform—they endure.

Thank you for engaging with these ideas. If this book has given you a more precise vocabulary, a sharper perspective, or the confidence to question conventional thinking, it has served its purpose.

The real work, as always, begins in practice.

About The Author

Asim Kumar Mukhopadhyay has been one of the foremost thought leaders on cost competitiveness, value creation, and enterprise leadership in India for over four decades. He has been part of the global automotive, Steel, mobility, and manufacturing industries, including several large conglomerates. Having spent much of his career within the Tata Group, including Senior leadership roles in Tata Motors and SAIL, he has worked at the heart of large, complex organizations where strategy, governance, and execution must align.

From the shop floor to the boardroom, he has led transformations that demanded discipline, clarity, and long-term thinking, introducing rigorous cost and performance frameworks while navigating sustainability, urban mobility, and organizational change. His work reflects a deep belief that value creation is not episodic, but systemic.

A chartered Accountant, a cost and management accountant, and a company secretary, recipient of many awards and accolades, including the Best CFO Award from India's premier accounting bodies. He was also recognized by the Ministry of Heavy Industries, Government of India, for his contribution to India's EV transformation. He is a lifetime fellow of the Institute of Directors. He has been conferred a Doctorate of Excellence (Honoris Causa) by the Confederation of International Accreditation Commission, in partnership with the

University of Entrepreneurship and Technology, USA (2019), in Finance Management.

He is associated with the Confederation of Indian Industries and has been an active member of its TCM Division for decades. Currently, he is a mentor of the CII TCM Division and a member of the CII Green Council.

Asim, who previously served as CEO & Managing Director of TML Smart City Mobility Solutions Ltd (a wholly owned subsidiary of Tata Motors, focused on an end-to-end e-mobility ecosystem), has held numerous senior leadership roles throughout his career. He is well respected for his ability to convert cost into capability and strategy into action. Today, Asim is also the founder and CEO of NAVTOM Consulting Pvt Ltd, where he advises boards and executives on building businesses that are clear, precise, and future-ready. Clarity Competes is a distillation of a career in leadership, encapsulated into a framework to provide businesses with an enduring competitive advantage.

www.ingramcontent.com/pod-product-compliance
Lightning Source LLC
Chambersburg PA
CBHW021656070726
47591CB00017B/511